T0361431

Quantum Safety

Quantum Safety

The New Approach to Risk Management for the Complex Workplace

Paul Stretton

Routledge
Taylor & Francis Group

A PRODUCTIVITY PRESS BOOK

First published 2022
by Routledge
605 Third Avenue, New York, NY 10158

and by Routledge
2 Park Square, Milton Park, Abingdon, Oxon, OX14 4RN

Routledge is an imprint of the Taylor & Francis Group, an informa business

ISBN: 978-1-032-00793-9 (hbk)
ISBN: 978-1-032-00792-2 (pbk)
ISBN: 978-1-003-17574-2 (ebk)

DOI: 10.4324/9781003175742

Typeset in Garamond
by Deanta Global Publishing Services, Chennai, India

Contents

List of Figures and Tables

Figures

Tables

Foreword

This book is an authoritative work which takes the reader on a journey towards a new perspective of safety in the workplace, the concept of Quantum Safety. It describes the evolution of safety thinking with stories and examples of the emerging concepts and ideology. It both reminds us of the journey we have been on, recognising the work that has been done before, and provides us with a refined model for the management of health and safety. Paul expertly builds each chapter, confronting his own thinking and that of others. We get to explore through his eyes the work of Erik Hollnagel, Sidney Dekker, Charles Vincent, Rene Amalberti, James Reason, Amy Edmondson, Steven Shorrock and many more.

People have been searching for a language and a model that could be used to describe the changes from the traditional safety methods to more enlightened new approaches to safety. For example, we have Safety I and Safety II and Safety Differently. Having a model helps communicate and explain. At the heart of the book is the new conceptual model of the Lilypond, which is used to bring to life the principles of Quantum Safety in the complex workplace.

The Lilypond helps us to visualise a complex system. From the surface level, it helps us to see the size and scale of the problem, and it helps us identify where the areas of learning are. From beneath the surface, we start to understand why the surface appears as it does. The model helps explain our systems in the form of an intricate ecosystem. We now know that none of our systems are neat or linear and that they are full of multiple interactions, interdependences, hierarchies, power imbalances and influences. This complexity impacts our every decision, action, behaviour and relationship. The Lilypond model helps us to consider these in detail.

All organisations are becoming more and more complex. The ability to maintain safety depends on the entrenched way we work within our current systems; the context, conditions and culture in which people try to work safely. These all dictate how organisations and the people within them are able to perform. Impacting the performance of complex work are the processes, the procedures, tasks, rules and directives that can both help and hinder. This book will urge you to understand this and provides the reader with tools and models to help organisations learn and improve, making the world a better and safer place.

Suzette Woodward

Professor Woodward is a visiting professor for the Institute of Global Health Innovation at Imperial College University London and honorary DSc at the University of West London. She is the author of a blog, numerous articles and two books: *Rethinking Patient Safety* and *Implementing Patient Safety*.

Preface

A spacecraft is the perfect Newtonian machine. By the time Apollo 11 landed on the moon on 16 July 1969, Newtonian physics, or classical mechanics, had described our understanding of the world and universe for nearly 300 years. As beautiful and brilliant as Newton's advances were, they were also incomplete. Newtonian physics could not be applied to the sub-atomic world. At this peculiar and complex level Newton doesn't work. This is the space for Quantum mechanics.

Quantum mechanics still confuses us. Theories that try to explain the mechanics are still widely debated and disputed by physicists. The relational interpretation of Quantum mechanics challenges the concept of physical systems with discrete items from planets to pebbles. Rather these objects do nothing in isolation but continuously act upon each other. Reality is a dense web of interactions.

The principles that describe our understanding of safety have hardly changed in 50 years. Like Newtonian physics, the advances have been real but the ideas are incomplete. In the modern complex workplace many of our traditional structures cease to work. Quantum Safety does not reject these legacy ideas entirely. Instead, we adopt a different perspective in order to create an understanding otherwise invisible to us. It is a move away from a linear mechanistic view of the science of work towards one that recognises reality is a dense web of interactions.

It is a privilege and honour to be able to share these ideas with you. The academic papers some of the chapters are based upon which have already been published have been widely well received. From aviation, healthcare and rail Quantum Safety has already begun to be embraced at organisational and national levels. What happens next depends on the reader and the interactions that follow reading this book.

To start with, in the first chapter we explore our Newtonian roots. This is our classical methodology that dominates most of our approaches to risk management. It is the perspective that explains the world of safety as we have understood it. We also look at the emerging alternatives approaches to safety, collectively called "New Views." Change is coming, but what that change will be is unclear.

In my opinion, embracing the insights provided by Complexity Science will revolutionise many walks of life. Areas such as public policy formulation and urban planning will be transformed. The opportunity to improve the science of work will also be significant. Quantum Safety introduces the importance of complexity in Chapter 2 and will be a consistent theme throughout this book.

The recognition of the importance of complexity renders our linear, Newtonian models obsolete. Bastions of our existing approaches, such as the Safety Triangle and Swiss Cheese Model, require a modern replacement. Chapter 3 introduces the new conceptual model for us to be able to understand our approaches to risk management in the modern, complex world. The model is expanded in Chapter 9 to explore the idea of causation within complex systems.

Systems thinking is also expanded within Quantum Safety. Too often defined approaches lead to tribalised absolutism. In Chapter 6 Quantum Safety eschews such intellectual linearity and develops a broader, more flexible concept of systems thinking for safety critical industries.

For Quantum Safety to be a catalyst for genuine transformation the reader requires more than conceptual models. Throughout this book concepts will be supported by ideas for application. Chapters 4 and 5 provide a mechanism to translate the conceptual model introduced into the world of work and a means to begin to explore the existing organisational performance in a manner in which existing maturity ladders or curves do not.

Chapter 7 introduces a new understanding of Just Culture, one that is appropriate for the modern, complex workplace. How the principles of Quantum Safety are embedded within an organisation via the language used is explored in Chapter 11 as traditional approaches to feedback and debriefing are replaced. In order to help bridge the application gap further, Chapters 8 and 10 provide examples across a range of safety critical industries so the reader can explore how Quantum Safety would manifest in their workplace further.

Finally, Chapter 12 will begin to encourage people to identify how they can transform their organisational approach to risk management in line with the principles established within Quantum Safety. It offers a refined model for the management of health and safety. Its outlines a future that empowers all people to become scientists of their own work, drive improvement and take ownership of their performance standards.

Author

Paul Stretton is a safety scientist having worked across high-risk industries developing safety leadership and culture change processes. He has published several papers in international academic literature developing progressive approaches to organisational safety. These works have already been implemented across a range of safety critical industries globally. *Quantum Safety* brings these concepts together, redefines how we consider safety and offers a future where people become scientists of their own work.

Acknowledgments

There are many people I want to thank who have helped me along my journey and the development of the ideas within this book. Firstly, I would like to thank Suzette Woodward. Her work in the NHS is incredible, and the support and advocacy she has offered me is something I shall always appreciate and never forget. Al Hellewell and Garin Underwood and everyone else within the Philosophical Breakfast Club for their enthusiasm and interest in my work as well as the initial groundwork that formed the basis of Chapter 4. Ben Tipney for championing my work and helping bring the ideas to teams across healthcare with the great work MedLed is doing, and Alistair Dunns, Simon Bown and Adam Johns for specific specialist input for some examples and early adoption of these principles. I would also like to thank Michael Sinocchi and Samantha Dalton at Taylor & Francis for helping bring this project to fruition. Finally, and most importantly, I would like to thank my parents for their support, and my brilliant wife, Cath, for being a permanent sounding board, critical friend, fierce supporter, companion and wonderful mother.

Finally, I would like to thank you for reading this. I hope you enjoy the journey as much as I have. Having said that, shall we get on with it?

Chapter 1

Newtonian Safety and the New View Refraction

Through this book we shall develop a different way of understanding safety in the workplace. This approach is Quantum Safety. It will challenge how we understand safety at a fundamental or philosophical level. For much of the early part of my career I simply accepted the concepts I had been taught and applied them. When I started to explore the notion of what I consider safety to be in the workplace, a whole new picture began to emerge. This book will take you on the same process of critical reflection and the creation of a new perspective of safety in the modern workplace.

This is not to say that our focus will be solely conceptual. The foundations are academic in nature, but too often real change is stymied due to the gap between theory and practice. This book bridges that gap by providing real-life examples and tools that can be used to implement the concepts offered within modern risk management systems. We will examine the principle of workplace safety with an entirely new approach and ask what, why, as well as how.

Before we begin this journey it is advantageous to reflect upon how our current understanding of safety became established as well as recognising more recent developments that attempt to provide alternative future pathways.

DOI: 10.4324/9781003175742-1

1.1 Newtonian Safety

Sir Isaac Newton, whilst self-isolating from a pandemic, experienced his annus mirabilis. His brilliance opened the door for an understanding of mechanics, calculus, optics and, of course, gravity.[1] The world today is still built largely on his work. Physics doesn't have a clear and obvious start point and is too broad an area to be dominated by one mind, even one with the genius of Newton. It is equally as impossible to place a date for the start point of safety. The industrial revolution of the mid-eighteenth century could be a reasonable place to start. Many have identified the role that safety played in Hammurabi's Code of Laws developed in the eighteenth century BC.[2] The need to preserve and perpetuate could be dated as far back as the rich primordial soup itself. Safety could easily be seen to be as innate and as omnipotent as classical scientific disciplines. It has been shaped by many great minds but owned by none.

The current notion of safety within the workplace is also a product of its own Newtonian moment. The Occupational Safety and Health Act was signed into law in 1970 by President Nixon. The Health and Safety at Work Act was followed in 1974 in Great Britain. These laws transformed safety in the same way that Newton transformed physics. The similarities between the two go beyond the scale of change they invoked. Indeed, much of our safety thinking during the 1970s was directly based on the intellectual structures of Newtonian physics.

The most basic principle within Newtonian Safety is to stop things from going wrong. The world that this creates is one we will all be familiar with. There are principles of prevention and assessments of risk. There are standard operating procedures and briefings. There are Safety Triangles and models with Swiss Cheese and Dominoes.[3-5] In due course all these will come under review as we explore the quantum realm of safety. It is this realm of Newtonian Safety in which people are developing alternative ways to understand workplace safety.

1.2 New Views

Quantum Safety is not the first proposed shift in our approach to organisational health and safety. There have been a number of alternative methodologies advanced. Cumulatively these advances have become known as New Views. Newtonian Safety has shone like a beaming ray of light into the workplace and now has struck a philosophical or intellectual prism. From the pure white light of Newtonian Safety, we now have refracted a spectrum of associated but differing approaches to understanding safety. It seems that a shift from Newtonian Safety is an idea whose time has come. What the shift is towards is not as clear. It would, therefore, be helpful to understand the kaleidoscopic New View landscape and the differing methodologies in order to consider how Quantum Safety converges with and diverges from these.

1.2.1 The First New View: Behaviour Based Safety

Behavioural-based safety (BBS) emerged as a popular approach to improving safety performance during the 1970s and 1980s.[6] BBS can be seen as the first philosophy that was developed to advance, complement and potentially challenge the Newtonian Safety world. There is not one homogenous approach to BBS and it has experienced numerous iterations over the years.

The theoretical underpinnings of BBS have been traced to Herbert Heinrich and his research during the 1930s. Within this research Heinrich suggested that 88% of accidents were caused by unsafe acts of persons, 10% by machine failure and 2% were unavoidable.[5] The notion that the human is the hazard was born.

The unsafe acts have subsequently been divided into errors; the unintended or substandard actions, and violations; deliberate deviations from known rules or procedures.[7] The application of these subtypes of human failure helped create the notion of "Zero Harm" and the goal of total safety perfection. The deliberate nature of violations means that such deliberate acts should be challenged and changed. If every person completely followed the rules and procedures, they will not come to harm or loss, provided that the rules and procedures are sufficient. This understanding of human behaviour is predicated on the idea of the economically rational agent, what Kahneman called "Homo Oeconomicus."[8] Through this lens people always act in a manner that maximises their utility or profit. It is a fine theory. It is elegant, simple and intuitive. Unfortunately, there is a problem with this view point to help improve safety: people are not rational agents.

Whilst BBS is not considered to be part of the current evolution of New Views of safety, it was the first attempt at thinking about safety in a different way. This demonstrates the desire for excellence inherent within risk management as well as tacit acknowledgment that Newtonian Safety on its own is not sufficient. The understanding of decision-making upon which such approaches are underpinned is often significantly outdated. The underlying belief that humans act in a rational manner is flawed and is also a frame from which a blame culture easily perpetuates. This is possibly why many organisations that have a behavioural based safety programme have evolved the concept into a more general approach to safety leadership, with varying quality and impact.

The traditional scope of BBS has not been universally well received. Many trade unions in particular have taken unfavourable stances regarding BBS. The Trade Union Congress (TUC) considers BBS to be "founded on a wrong premise," namely the act of the worker rather than the role of management in unsafe acts or conditions.[9] In 2011, Workers Uniting which consists of The United Steel Workers Union and Unite, Britain and Ireland's largest union, stated their opposition to BBS as they "shift the blame for accidents and poor health & safety from management to workers."[10]

1.2.2 Safety II

Eric Hollnagel proposed the concept of Safety II.[11] Hollnagel called the Newtonian Safety that we introduced at the beginning of this chapter Safety I, where the concept of safety is defined by the notion of as few things as possible going wrong. In contrast, Safety II considers safety to be defined by the notion of as many things as possible going right. In so doing, Hollnagel created a dichotomy in terms of what we consider to be safety in the workplace. This alternative start point represents a significant shift in how we attempt to understand organisational performance.

This shift has been explained in a number of ways. A common analogy is to consider whether anyone would be tempted to buy a golf coaching book called "101 missed putts" as opposed to "My 101 best putts." This fixation on failure is an instinctive frame for Newtonian Safety. The value in contrast to learning from what goes well is clear. If someone wishes to achieve something they would automatically look at how other people achieve it. They would not immediately look to see how they had failed.

A more in-depth explanation of Safety II that is frequently offered is the work of Abraham Wald. Wald was a mathematician who made a significant breakthrough for the Allied forces.[12] Engineers were routinely provided with a statistical overview of where planes were most usually damaged the most. This identified areas of the aircraft that required additional strengthening. Wald identified a flaw in this analysis. Wald proposed that the Navy implement a strategy that was the exact opposite. The data was based upon planes that were able to return, whereas many were not as successful. Wald reasoned that this was because the planes that returned had not been as severely damaged and so the places to strengthen on the aircraft were where the data showed no impacts. If a plane got hit in one of those areas, it meant it was not able to return at all. It is an analogy that is helpful to encourage people to reflect on the information they have about performance. The information, however, may not help us to become more successful without a wider consideration of context. As a strict example to advocate a Safety II approach the validity is less clear. The Navy had been learning from relative success and were ignorant to the true nature of failure. As soon as the Navy understood the true nature of the risks to the aircraft they could improve. It was, however, a useful point of divergence when developing the concept of Quantum Safety. Too often our approach to safety is predicated by the outcome.

Safety II is not solely interested in recognising and understanding safety through a positive lens. Hollnagel advances a number of alternative ideas regarding causation and the role of humans. For example, he states that humans can provide flexibility within a system that creates resilience and potentially have a positive impact on safety outcomes. This is a significant change from considering humans to be hazards as classical behavioural approaches proposed. A more nuanced understanding of the relationship between the person and the system emerges.

Safety II has challenged many paradigms that previously seemed fixed and is rightly considered to be very important work in developing our approaches to risk management. How organisations translate the principles developed by Hollnagel is less clear. Frequently organisations try to repurpose their Safety I methodology to Safety II with mixed success. Quantum Safety develops some of the ideas Hollnagel introduces in Safety II, as well as addressing the challenges he effectively outlines with Newtonian Safety.

1.2.3 Safety Differently

Safety Differently is another powerful brand within the New View of safety developed by Sidney Dekker.[13] The philosophical underpinning of this view is heavily based on Hollnagel's work regarding viewing safety through an approach of understanding what works well and why. Safety Differently defines safety "as capacity to be successful in varying conditions." Dekker also advances that "people are a solution to enable or facilitate." Safety Differently focuses on the adaptive behaviours of people within the system and considers this variation to create resilience in the system which is often crucial in creating successful outcomes, in a similar manner to the argument developed by Hollnagel.

One aspect of Safety Differently that is noticeably different to Safety II is in the provision of a route for application. Dekker considers Safety Differently to be a revised mental model of safety where organisations learn from normal work and engage with workers exposed to the risks to identify appropriate ways to manage the risks. Whilst the idea of workforce engagement could hardly be considered to be a new principle within safety management, the more holistic view of organisational safety combined with a concept of grass roots change is an approach that has garnered traction across a number of industries for good reason.

1.2.4 Safety III

Safety III is a newcomer to the New View market. It has been proposed by Professor Nancy Leveson from MIT in 2020.[14] The article "Safety III: A systems approach to safety and resilience" was written largely as a direct critique of Hollnagel's Safety II. Leveson offers a definition of safety within Safety III as "as freedom from unacceptable losses as identified by the system stakeholders. The goal is to eliminate, mitigate, or control hazards, which are the states that can lead to these losses." This definition is closer to the Newtonian Safety world as it is based around failure avoidance and so Safety III should not be considered to be a progression of Safety II methodology. Safety III is more of modernisation or revisitation of Newtonian Safety. This does not mean Safety III does not have anything valuable to offer. It is, however, a significantly more limited view of safety than the one developed within Quantum Safety.

Whilst most of Safety III is a focused critique of Safety II, to the point where at times it can feel like the reader is intruding on a failed marriage counselling session, there are a number of interesting principles proposed that this book shall explore further. The primacy given to understanding the system, systems thinking, is helpful. As is the recognition of the weakness of linear approaches and the rejection of the concept of a root cause. These are developed comprehensively within Quantum Safety. In the main, Safety III redefines what Newtonian/Safety I is from an engineering perspective rather than proposing a new paradigm in safety thinking and risk management.

One of Leveson's many critiques of Hollnagel's Safety II is the central role people play within it. We will develop the role of systems and people in

Chapter 6. Additionally, Leveson consistently makes the distinction between product/system safety and workplace safety as well as a reference to engineers and engineering in contrast to people and work. It is not clear how this further fragmentation and creation of silos is helpful or valid. Whilst different characteristics manifest dependent on the particular perspective at any one time, for a philosophical approach to be worthwhile these differing characteristics should be accounted for. There has not been a sufficiently convincing argument made that warrants product safety, system safety, workplace safety, patient safety, road safety, etc. to have their own pseudo-scientific branch. Throughout this book we shall consider the arguments and criticisms made within both Safety II and Safety III as we understand more deeply the science of work.

1.3 The New View Landscape

The current New View landscape is an increasingly competitive environment. At times it can even be a little hostile. The definition of safety itself is not fixed. Hollnagel, Dekker and Leveson all define safety in different ways. The importance of systems and the role of people within them at times are diametrically opposed dependent on which New View is being considered. The classical, Newtonian approach to safety continues to forge its path of white light. Upon hitting the prism we can now place the differing New Views. The least refracted view, sporting a rather red hue, would be Leveson's Safety III. It remains wedded to the avoidance of failure as a guiding principle, but with a simplistic and possibly more realistic understanding of systems to help achieve it. Next there are behavioural-based approaches to safety, depending on exactly their ethos and overall goals. More traditional behavioural approaches seek to gain greater compliance of the workforce behaviours within the system. Rational humans can reduce their variation and cease becoming a hazard. There are some initiatives which are considered to still be behaviourally based but have a different understanding of the role people play within systems and what the organisation wishes to prioritise or change.

Safety II has refracted further still and finds itself nearer the blue end of the colour spectrum. Safety is no longer only concerned with avoiding failure and people can provide solutions not just problems. Finally, Safety Differently shares much of Safety II's philosophical refraction, but with a deeper sense of how this manifests within organisations.

1.4 Moving into the Quantum World

The New View refraction is exciting and inspiring. There is a lot of fantastic work undertaken by brilliant people who are passionate about improving the world of work. There is a clear desire for many people to modernise our view of organisational safety. This should not be surprising given how much the nature of work has evolved since the main principles of Newtonian Safety became established across risk industries. But it has also created a range of ideas that are incohesive at best and in conflict at worst.

Firstly, the choice of nomenclature, whilst doubtless well intentioned and logical at the moment of their coining, creates confusion and bemusement in equal measure. Safety I, Safety II and now Safety III lead people to naturally wonder when Safety IV will be offered. This creates a frame where organisational safety will receive periodic upgrades; safety as another consumer product like a smartphone or games console.

For those that strongly advocate a New View there is also a significant flaw. In particular, disciples of Safety II and Safety Differently approaches struggle to address one basic and obvious fact – Newtonian Safety works. It works incredibly well. Failing to recognise the success of Newtonian Safety and the many years of work that has underpinned this may explain the ire evident in some of the writing within Safety III. Any New View that fails to recognise this progress can only be severely weakened as a result. The suggestion of people becoming "safety anarchists" should be considered as misguided as it is disrespectful.

The source of this conflict and confusion stems from the fact that with all of the views outlined, we are still essentially in the Newtonian world of safety. That is to say that despite the efforts and excellence, the focus is still on trying to understand the nature of light. Analysing whether our beam has been refracted and by how much will offer insights into the nature of light as a whole, but it will not offer a view that is truly new or transformative. To do that we need to leave the realm of Newtonian Safety and begin to consider the world at a quantum level. Newtonian physics was able to get man on the moon, but it required our understanding of quantum mechanics to provide the platform to enable us to do so. In a similar manner we need to consider safety from an entirely new perspective. A perspective that does not invalidate its Newtonian cousins or create false dichotomies.

Welcome to Quantum Safety. And all of its complexity.

Question for Reflection

By its very nature, is it imperative that our understanding of safety be based upon the idea of failure avoidance? Or does an approach that is predicated on creating the conditions for the best, optimal performance enable progress that a failure avoidance focus alone would not?

References

1. White M. (1998). *Isaac Newton: The Last Sorcerer.* Harper Collins.
2. Hale A & Hovden J. (1998). Management and culture: The third age of safety. A review of approaches to organisational aspects of safety, health and environment. In *Occupational Injury: Risk, Prevention and Intervention.* Taylor & Francis.
3. Heinrich HW. (1931). *Industrial Accident Prevention: A Scientific Approach.* McGraw-Hill.
4. Reason J. (1990). *Human Error.* Cambridge University Press.
5. Heinrich HW. (1941). *Industrial Accident Prevention. A Scientific Approach* (2nd ed.). New York & London: McGraw-Hill Book Company, Inc.
6. Anderson M. (2005). Behavioural safety and major accident hazards. A magic bullet or shot in the dark? *Process Safety and Environmental Protection,* 83(B2): 109–116.
7. Reason J. (1997). *Managing the Risks of Organisational Accidents.* Ashgate.
8. Kahneman D. (2011). *Thinking Fast and Slow.* Strauss and Giroux.
9. Trade Union Congress. (2010). Behavioural safety: A briefing for workplace representatives. [online] Available at: https://www.tuc.org.uk/sites/default/files/BehaviouralSafety.pdf [Accessed 12.03.21].
10. United Steel Workers. (2010). Behavior-based safety/blame the work safety programs. Understanding and confronting managements plan for workplace health and safety. [online] Available at: https://images.usw.org/conv2011/convention2011/healthsafety/Confronting%20Blame%20the%20Worker%20Safety%20Programs%20Book%20April%202010.pdf [Accessed 12.03.21].
11. Hollnagel E. (2014). *Safety-I and Safety-II. The Past and Future of Safety Management.* CRC Press.
12. Mangel M & Samaniego FJ. (1984). Abraham Wald's work on aircraft survivability. *Journal of the American Statistical Association,* 79: 259–267.
13. Dekker S. (2014). *Safety Differently: Human Factors for a New Era.* CRC Press.
14. Leveson N. (2020). *Safety III: A Systems Approach to Safety and Resilience.* MIT Press.

Chapter 2

Let's Talk about Complexity

Most people will have heard that "safety is just common sense" at some point. Some may even have thought it. It is as understandable as it is incorrect. Safety is not just common sense. Sometimes safety may be simple. To ensure our approach to risk management is suitable for the modern workplace we need to shun the common-sense mantra and understand the nature of complexity. Quantum Safety was developed from this understanding.

The term "complexity" is used with ever greater frequency. As often happens with workplace jargon, the true meaning of the term can quickly become diluted or lost. This has also occurred with Safety II[1] where Hollnagel's work is understood by some as an approach that only learns from best practice. Complexity, as the mot de jour in many risk management circles, becomes misunderstood or misapplied; for example, as a recent paper from the Chartered Institute of Ergonomics and Human Factors (CIEHF) stated, "in clinical settings, having a good understanding of the complexity of the work system is sometimes described as 'situational awareness.'"[2] Complexity has become a synonym for difficult and is as accurate as substituting Safety II with the idea of learning from best practice.

Complexity Science can put people off. By nature it's not exactly straightforward. This may explain why the term is used inaccurately or loosely. It also challenges the way we try to understand the world of work. This does not mean that the concept of complexity has to be difficult to embrace. Indeed, it is imperative that Complexity Science is truly embraced in order to utilise the valuable implications to risk management that it offers. Quantum

DOI: 10.4324/9781003175742-2

Safety, therefore, appropriately adopts Einstein's maxim that "everything should be made as simple as possible, but no simpler."[3]

2.1 Different Types of Systems

By introducing the idea of complexity we are beginning to acknowledge that different systems of work behave differently. They have different characteristics and consequently the way we manage risk within them needs to become more flexible. These different characteristics are often neatly split into three broad types of system: simple, complicated and complex.[4]

Simple systems are the domain of cause and effect. Simple systems have an established system of best practice with few variables to manage. Irrespective of who is doing the work the outcome remains consistent, provided the system is followed. Someone following a basic recipe such as making a cup of coffee would be working within a simple system. So too a referee replacing the coloured balls during a game of snooker. Having potted a red ball a player is entitled to pot one of the coloured balls. The referee then places the ball back on its preordained spot. There are additional rules for situations where it is not possible to relocate the ball on its spot to prevent the game from unravelling in certain situations. These systems are both simple and excellent.

A series of simple systems can be accumulated to form a complicated system. There is a greater range of actions being undertaken and so the role of expertise and coordination becomes more important. Crucially though, once a formula has been found for success this can be replicated multiple times irrespective of who is within the system, provided they are suitably trained.

A Formula One pit stop would be a good example of a complicated system. The task has a high degree of technical difficulty and the engineers within the teams are highly trained. The results they achieve are brilliant. The pit stop system can be broken down into a series of component parts and reassembled with relative ease. Changes in personnel within the team, provided they are competent, will not significantly impact the overall pit stop as the engineers are essentially acting as important cogs in a well-oiled machine. Despite there being a large number of people involved within the system, a strict view of system dynamics would not consider it to be a complex system.

There sometimes seems to be a desire for one's own system to be considered complex rather than complicated as a result of an inferred superiority.

This is unhelpful and misguided. There is no inference regarding the quality or importance of work carried out in either type of system dynamics. There is, however, an important consequence for the management of risk within the systems.

Complex systems possess different characteristics. An article in *Harvard Business Review* explains that

> a complex adaptive system has three characteristics. The first is that the system consists of a number of heterogeneous agents, and each of those agents makes decisions about how to behave. The most important dimension here is that those decisions will evolve over time. The second characteristic is that the agents interact with one another. That interaction leads to the third—something that scientists call emergence: In a very real way, the whole becomes greater than the sum of the parts. The key issue is that you can't really understand the whole system by simply looking at its individual parts.[5]

I appreciate that this is a kind of language that can alienate many people and so shall adopt Einstein's principle to explain Complexity Science.

Complex systems are shaped largely by relationships. Any system, therefore, with a large number of people could be considered complex to some degree; the greater the degree of interconnectivity the greater the level of complexity. (This is why the Formula One pit stop crew would be considered to be a complicated system, not complex, as the people work with as minimal interaction as possible when executing the task.) These people are almost entirely well intentioned and work to find the best outcome. In complex systems, individual actions or decisions cannot be learnt from in isolation. This is analogous to playing a game of Rock, Paper, Scissors. It is impossible to analyse whether someone's decision to select paper is optimal, without taking into consideration the other person's decision, understood as non-equilibrium dynamics.[6] Within such dynamics small variations from the equilibrium can produce significant differences in the state of the system. Unfortunately, the best outcome is not obvious often and so people accept what they consider to be good enough. This becomes more difficult as people often have to satisfy different masters or competing goals. People want to make decisions that are safe. They also need to make decisions that are profitable, productive and get the job completed. What people consider to be acceptable will change and will also be affected by decisions other people have made separately. Understanding the effect of these interactions is hugely important.

Team sports are good examples of complex systems. Whether watching FC Barcelona mesmerises opponents, or the New Zealand All Blacks carve through a defence, we are watching the result of countless interactions and decisions within a complex system. People are adapting and trying to achieve a successful outcome without one obvious clear option to take. Changing one player can, and often does, significantly change how the system performs. Studying the individual players in isolation will not provide much insight into how the team will perform.

2.2 Systems, Complexity and Emergence

At this point, it should not be a huge surprise that there are limitations in applying such a clear delineation of system properties to the messy reality of the modern workplace. It is one thing to recognise that the system that enables a referee to replace a snooker ball is different from a Formula One pit stop and that both are very different again to how an elite rugby team functions. It is another thing to consider how these different system properties impact how we manage risk.

Consider a bricklayer on a construction site. What kind of system would they be working within? One view would be to consider their work as an example of a simple system. The laying of bricks is essentially following a recipe with the relationship between cause and effect clear. The bricklayer may be part of a team of bricklayers or other construction workers, compiling their simple systems to make the overall system more complicated. There would also be a plausible argument that on large construction projects we see multiple teams of specialist workers, several layers of management hierarchy within which exist particular differing areas of priority ranging from commercial, customer relations, production, safety and environmental factors. Each person within this system, including our bricklayer, would be making what they thought to be the best decision at the time of making it. What is the optimal decision is not necessarily clear given the conflicting demands people are under, and emergent behaviour can occur. The bricklayer is now working within a system with complex characteristics similar to those the New Zealand All Blacks work within.

The characteristics we observe and the behaviour of the system, therefore, are not one fixed concept. A system is not just categorised as simple, complicated or complex. The system can display different characteristics dependent upon the perspective of the person viewing. This may be a challenging principle to accept by some safety scientists and those interested in organisational behaviour, but there is a sound scientific basis for this principle of multifaceted systemic behaviours. From Robert Hooke, in 1665, when studying the spread of light, to Michael Faraday in 1847 linking light to electro-magnetism, light was considered to have wave-like properties. In 1900 Max Plank described light as being constituted of lumps of energy, quanta. This insight of light allowed Einstein to propose the theory of photoelectric effect. Quantum mechanics now recognises that light can be described as either a wave or a particle dependent on the perspective and the insight required. Light can be considered to have wave-like properties or be constituted of particles depending on the perspective adopted, and with similar intellectual nimbleness the systemic characteristics may shift as our analytical view shifts.

In Safety III, Leveson dismisses the validity of Complexity Science, stating the belief "that Complexity Theory frameworks provide a poor basis for the goals related to improving safety and other emergent system properties in engineered socio-technical systems."[7] Leveson advocates Systems Theory, which shares many similarities. The reason Leveson offers for the distinction is that Systems Theory allows for emergence to occur in non-complex systems. It is also worthy to note that Leveson argues that Complexity Theory is only really appropriate to natural systems, not man-made ones. This is a surprising claim given the wide range of published research using complexity within man-made systems, including traffic routes, dating and financial crashes.[8] The previous example of the systemic properties that will affect the bricklayer provides room for both recognising the importance of complexity and emergence within systems that may not be considered to be complex within traditional, prescriptive delineations.

In a similar manner to how complexity is inappropriately used to describe work that is difficult, emergence is often used as a synonym for unexpected. So when people say they observe emergence in a complex system, they really mean that unexpected behaviours occur when work is difficult. Emergence, whilst ill defined, means more than unexpected.

Emergence can be an output of the system (phenemonological emergence). This is an "observable instance, emergence is an interesting and unpredicted pattern, behaviour or otherwise of a system."[9] These unexpected effects are a result of interactions between people or parts of the system. Emergence can also be considered to be a characteristic of the system itself (ontological emergence). This emergence is one where the system displays a characteristic that means understanding, causes and explanations at a micro level do not apply at a macro level and vice versa.

Consider the example of the All Blacks. A lot of their play will be a result of well-rehearsed patterns executed by incredibly skilled practitioners. This will be delivered on systems that have been designed following in-depth analysis and coached by people as good as any in the industry. There may be, however, a certain passage of play during a rugby game that was unexpected or had an unpredicted pattern. The players reacted to a specific situation that created an outcome entirely different from the pre-game expectations. This would be emergence as an output (phenomenological). Emergence is most commonly considered in these terms when applied to risk management.

We could contrast this to the dynamics we observe when viewing the governance of major events. The president of the United States of America could be considered to be a leader of a very complex system. In 1962 the world came as close as it ever has to a nuclear holocaust during the Cuban Missile Crisis. The events of the 13 days of the Cuban Missile Crisis provide an excellent example of how a complex system can behave. The objectives were not clear, aside from the avoidance of global destruction. There was never a clear optimal decision to take and results were determined once other people within the system had also made a decision. Such was the rich interconnectivity of decision-making that if any one person was replaced by another, if John F. Kennedy was not president, or if any of the pilots flying missions over Cuba been different, it is quite possible the outcome would've been different, possibly significantly and tragically so. There was no clear emergent phenomenon that allowed the world to keep peace during those 13 days, rather the emergence was a property of the system itself (ontological).

The month prior to the Cuban Missile Crisis, President Kennedy gave one of his most memorable speeches, announcing that the USA would get a man on the moon before the end of the decade. The Apollo Program that followed was a vast, expensive system creating work of the greatest imaginable importance. In Chapter 1 we noted that the Apollo Program was successful due to Newtonian physics. It also needed the breakthroughs of quantum physics to create the computational power. This scientific relationship of differing fields or perspectives is congruent to those of system dynamics considered here. The Apollo Program is widely used as an example of a complicated system. The difficulty and importance of the work do not mean it is complex. Apollo was successful as a result of highly skilled, specialist engineers working on specific tasks which, once assembled, took human-kind to the moon. The systemic dynamics, therefore, share much more similarity with the Formula One pit crew than the Cuban Missile Crisis.

There are a broad spectrum of behaviours and characteristics within socio-technical systems observable in the modern workplace. These characteristics can be dynamic and less easy to categorise than some academics propose. There is no optimal level of complexity for a system to adopt. The nature of complexity within the system and the consequential degree of emergence is a foundational level of understanding upon which our risk management approach can be developed. This shall be explored in more depth in Chapter 6.

2.3 Complexity Law and Order

Professor Mary Uhl-Bien has developed an interesting framework for leadership within complex systems, Complexity Leadership Theory, which helps explain common approaches to risk management, as well as how they may in some instances be flawed. Complexity Leadership Theory proposes "that adaptability, which enhances performance and innovation, occurs in the everyday interactions of individuals acting in response to pressures and opportunities in their local contexts."[10] However, "in many organizations, these linkages are hard to make because of organizational bureaucracy and silos." The interconnectivity required is stifled. This occurs due to tension inherent within the system between the desire to produce and the desire to innovate. The tension will always be present, but how the organisation responds to it should be dictated by the system dynamics present.

The most typical response is a desire for order and control. When the tension between production and innovation is observed, leaders tend to respond by managing, or reducing, the tension. This is often achieved by stymying the innovation and asserting a degree of control or order on the system. This can lead to another layer of management or process bureaucratization. There will be many organisations whose safety management system has evolved from a multitude of order responses to potential adaptation, especially in industries where variation is considered to be a weakness that needs to be eradicated. This order response is appropriate for a complicated system, but not in a complex one. This can be seen frequently in organisational responses to accidents. The organisation often wishes to apply a greater sense of control on the task that has failed which results in an additional layer of a safe system of work. This could be an additional permit, checklist or mandatory PPE requirements.

Alternatively, one can respond to an issue arising from complexity with a solution based within complexity. This is what Boisot and McKelvey call the "law of requisite complexity."[11] This means creating space for adaptive thought and innovations that are able to work with the inherent tension between the need to produce and the desire to improve. Rather than the hierarchical top-down approach to change, multidisciplinary networks can more effectively work towards a different, viable future. Within Safety Differently there have been case studies cited that have adopted an approach that moves from a top-down approach.[12] The changes occurred as a result of a mechanism which resembles the idea of multidisciplinary adaptive space, although the similarities appear serendipitous rather than deliberate.

This is an approach that the All Blacks and other high-performing organisations have utilised to great success. Some progressive NHS trusts have also begun to develop performance hubs or networks that adopt this new way of improving approaches to managing risk. This approach may feel uncomfortable as the power gradients become shallower and progress is not always a smooth trajectory. It is, however, a fundamental shift in understanding how we work, how we learn and how we improve our approach to managing risk.

Embracing the different system dynamics, the modern workplace experience is crucial to creating improvement and an optimal safety performance. How we try to implement change within those systems will need to reflect the system dynamics that are present. Some solutions can be simple. Some may require to be discharged through a hierarchy. Others will need greater flexibility and innovation which can be discouraged or stopped with traditional approaches to risk management. It should, however, not be a surprise that existing approaches to risk management are predicated on linear thinking when our models of safety are still based on the linear Newtonian Safety world. A new approach will require a new conceptual framework to work within.

Questions for Reflection

1. What is the nature of complexity within your organisation?
2. How often are complex problems addressed with an order-based approach?
3. Where are adaptive spaces within your organisation?

References

1. Hollnagel E. (2014). *Safety-I and Safety-II. The Past and Future of Safety Management*. CRC Press.
2. Chartered Institute of Ergonomics & Human Factors. (2020). Coping with complexity. [online] Available at https://www.ergonomics.org.uk/Common/Uploaded%20files/Publications/CIEHF%20Coping%20with%20complexity.pdf [Accessed 19.01.21].
3. Sargut G & Gunther McGrath R. (2010). Managing under complexity: Where is Einstein when you really need him? *Ivey Business Journal*. [online] Available at: https://www.researchgate.net/profile/Goekce_Sargut/publication/27577197 5_Managing_Under_Complexity_Where_is_Einstein_When_You_Really_Nee d_Him/links/5572045308ae7521586717ae/Managing-Under-Complexity-Where-is-Einstein-When-You-Really-Need-Him.pdf [Accessed 21.01.21].
4. Glouberman S & Zimmerman B. (2002). *Complicated and Complex Systems: What Would Successful Reform of Medicare Look Like? Discussion Paper no 8 Commission on the Future of Health Care in Canada*. [online] Available at: https://www.researchgate.net/profile/Sholom_Glouberman/publication/265240426_Complicated_and_Complex_Systems_What_Would_Successful _Reform_of_Medicare_Look_Like/links/548604670cf268d28f044afd/Complicate d-and-Complex-Systems-What-Would-Successful-Reform-of-Medicare-Look-Like.pdf?origin=publication_detail [Accessed 21.01.21].
5. Sullivan T. (2011). Embracing complexity. *Harvard Business Review*. [online] Available at: https://hbr.org/2011/09/embracing-complexity [Accessed 21.01.21].
6. Sinervo B & Lively, CM. (1996). The rock-paper-scissors game and the evolution of alternative male strategies. *Nature*, 380: 240–243.
7. Leveson N. (2020). *Safety III: A Systems Approach to Safety and Resilience*. MIT Press.
8. Johnson N. (2007). *Simply Complexity: A Clear Guide to Complexity Theory*. Oneworld Publications.
9. Johnson, JJ, Tolk, A, Sousa-Poza, A. (2013). A theory of emergence and entropy in systems of systems. *Procedia Computer Science*. 20:283–289.
10. Uhl-Bien M & Arena M. (2017). Complexity leadership: Enabling people and organisations for adaptability. *Organizational Dynamics*, 46(1): 9–20.
11. Boisot M & Mckelvey B. (2011). Complexity and organization-environment relations: Revisiting Ashby's law of requisite variety. In Peter Allen, Steve Maguire & Bill McKelvey (eds.), *The Sage Handbook of Complexity and Management*. Sage Publications. pp. 279–298.
12. Dekker, S. (2014). *Safety Differently: Human Factors for a new era*. CRC Press.

Chapter 3

The Lilypond: A New Conceptual Model to Understand Safety Performance in the Modern, Complex Workplace

The Newtonian Safety world has provided us with many models to understand safety. These models have become ubiquitous in risk management syllabuses. Safety management systems are developed, either directly or indirectly, upon the understanding of safety that the models provide. It is also important to recognise that these models have contributed hugely to our understanding and improvements for more than half a century. James Reason's Swiss Cheese Model (SCM) was developed in 1990, and Heinrich's Safety Triangle was first published in 1931. Since the development of these models, our workplaces are more complex, our use of technology has transformed our practices and societal awareness of emotional and psychological health has increased dramatically. It should not be unreasonable that these seminal models have come under increasing review and critique from Safety Scientists. James Reason himself identified limitations with his model. For example, Luxhoj and Kauffeld write: "One of the disadvantages of the Reason model is that it does not account for the detailed interrelationships among causal factors. Without these distinct linkages, the results are too vague to be of significant practical use."[1] Despite this critique, the

DOI: 10.4324/9781003175742-3

traditional models are almost exclusively used, thus anchoring our approach to risk management within the Newtonian world. It is not possible to create Quantum Safety using old tools.

The Lilypond Model is one of the new tools. It conceptualises the principles of Quantum Safety in the complex workplace. This is not the first time such a model has been proposed. Edgar Schein discussed a Lilypond Model where visible manifestations are arrived at by values below the surface, rooted by underlying assumptions.[2] Whilst this Lilypond Model has been developed independently, the fact that biological systems are used to provide a conceptual framework for understanding complexity in man-made, socio-technical systems seems both immediate and accessible.

There are two views of the Lilypond, both of which are vital for understanding basic principles within Quantum Safety and will develop some of the ideas proposed by Erik Hollnagel and Safety II.[3] The first is a view of the surface from above. The second is a cross-sectional view through the Lilypond.

3.1 The View from Above

3.1.1 Outcome Representation

Traditionally, safety outcomes have been presented within Heinrich's Safety Triangle[4] (see Figure 3.1).

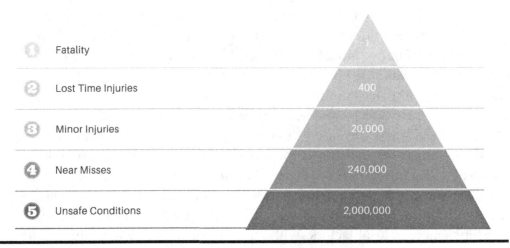

Safety Performance Triangle

①	Fatality	1
②	Lost Time Injuries	400
③	Minor Injuries	20,000
④	Near Misses	240,000
⑤	Unsafe Conditions	2,000,000

Figure 3.1   The Safety Triangle (adapted from Heinrich[4]).

Hollnagel critiques the choice to present this data in a triangle, as it misleads the reader into inferring a relationship of causation. A near miss is defined as "an event not causing harm, but has the potential to cause injury or ill health."[5] A near miss is often described as being the last stop before harm occurs. It is better to address the near miss than wait for the unsafe condition to actualise. The conventional wisdom is that an organisation should desire to identify and record as many near misses as possible, as this will result in a reduction in the number of more major adverse outcomes. It is a simple, intuitive logic that is appealing. It is also unfortunately severely flawed.

The inference created representing the data in a triangle is that both the near miss and the fatality share the same cause. The research conducted by Heinrich, however, only demonstrated a proportional relationship, not a causal one.[4] The widely accepted presentation and resultant interpretation of these data are, therefore, incorrect. A near miss, by nature, is a high likelihood–low severity outcome. A fatality is the opposite. The dynamics behind these events is, therefore, likely to be very different, yet our Newtonian understanding expects them to be the same.

Hollnagel describes the most ideal way to represent different severities of adverse events would be as a series of unrelated circles.[3] This removes the inference of causality within the Safety Triangle. The Lilypond Model extends this idea. Whilst it is important to challenge a frame of a direct causal relationship, it is possible that different adverse events may be related. To separate them entirely is, therefore, as flawed as to expect them to have the same dynamics behind them.

Every adverse event is a product of the organisational system. The Lilypond Model places each adverse event as lily pads floating on the surface of the pond, which vary in size based on the frequency of their occurrence (see Figure 3.2). This allows the adverse events to be related to each other directly by the root or associatively by recognising they are all products of the same system; the ecosystem within the Lilypond will impact multiple lily pads. The Lilypond does not consider adverse events to be isolated and discrete.

For example, in a hospital setting, an increase in near miss reporting may indicate that there is a high potential for patients having slips, trips and falls, which may or may not share any direct cause with a healthcare worker losing time to work due to a serious back injury. Newtonian thinking using the Safety Triangle would suggest that the more near misses of falls reported, the fewer serious adverse events that occur. On initial investigation, these

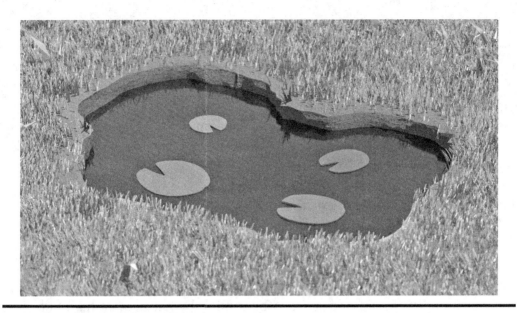

Figure 3.2 The Lilypond: adverse outcomes.

two adverse events do not share the same cause, but because they are products of the same Lilypond there may be an indirect linking factor. For example, lack of suitable hoisting equipment may be a current within the Lilypond that has contributed to both adverse outcomes.

The Safety Triangle only measures adverse events. As this research was conducted during the 1930s, this should be expected such was the view of organisational safety. The Lilypond has only a small number of different-sized lily pads on the surface, which reflects this perspective of safety. Safety II challenges the convention of only measuring and valuing adverse events.[3] The same system that creates the adverse events also creates a far higher number of successful events. If the lily pads already on the pond represent adverse events, we colour them black. There are many more white pads; these are successful events. The Lilypond Model allows for a more realistic and healthier view of workplace performance because it focuses on all outcomes: the 95% which are white and successful as well as the 5% that are black and unsuccessful (see Figure 3.3).

3.1.2 A Non-monochrome World

So far, we have a Lilypond covered with a majority of white lily pads and a small number of black lily pad outcomes, all proportionally sized by outcome frequency. The Lilypond Model recognises that our organisational

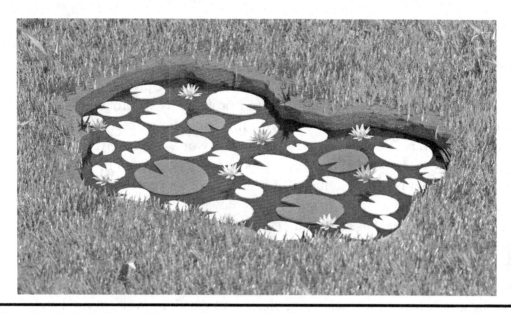

Figure 3.3   The Lilypond integrating Safety I and Safety II.

outcomes are more complex than that. Within every performance spectrum, there will be excellence grading through to poor performance. The Lilypond Model recognises the importance of acknowledging excellence as part of a high-performance culture. Out of the 95% of white lily pads, some will be the very best: the optimal, the brilliant and the most beautiful. These too need to be measured, valued and analysed. If there is an opportunity to learn from the worst possible outcomes, there should equally be opportunities to learn valuable lessons from successful events.[6]

This principle has sometimes been incorrectly conflated with Safety II. Learning from positive outcomes is a principle developed within Safety II; it is not Safety II of itself. Within the NHS, there has been a concerted effort to introduce Learning from Excellence systems. The same as other safety-critical industries, healthcare has incident reporting systems. A dedicated and interested group of frontline workers, inspired by the work of Erik Hollnagel and Safety II, created an alternative, complementary system that enables teams to identify, share and learn from best practices and important innovations. The black lily pads are no longer the only things that are recognised or valued.

Whilst some organisations are increasingly valuing and learning from best practices, it is significantly underutilised when considering safety performance. For example, I was supporting a small, but rapidly growing construction firm. They were working on a project for Network Rail. During some remediation works on an embankment, it became clear that the land was potentially contaminated with asbestos. The project manager raised the concern with his superiors to ascertain the correct, safe way about proceeding with the works. Despite there being some pressure from senior leaders concerned about productivity and profitability to proceed with less diligence, the project manager insisted on getting the correct information and developed a safe way of carrying out the work. Ultimately, the remediation work was completed safely and satisfactorily. Serendipitously, the project was also completed ahead of time and more profitably than forecast, as a result of savings made from waste removal, made possible from the work as carried out. I asked what actions had been taken subsequently in terms of reporting and learning. This seemed to be a difficult concept to grasp. Asked what would have happened if the work had been carried out unsafely and people, potentially members of the public, had been exposed to asbestos, a litany of procedures, alerts and reactions were immediately offered. Our Newtonian view of safety is too often reactionary as it is founded on the principle of failure avoidance. The limitation of this mental anchor is clear as this instance demonstrates. In Newtonian Safety, the only outcomes that are particularly valued, measured and reacted to are the black lily pads.

A balanced approach to measuring and learning from all outcomes would be a powerful shift in our risk management approach. It does, however, still utilise some vestiges from the traditional Newtonian approach. Newtonian Safety applies value judgements to work outcomes, which then bias all subsequent analysis and investigation. When an adverse event is identified, our behaviour is primed with a desire to right the wrong for those affected and apportion blame. Likewise, for successful outcomes, the most beautiful lily pads, the excellence is rightfully celebrated, but we are at risk of tacitly accepting or ignoring aspects of poor practice within the process. The "score" drives our analysis of the performance. Newtonian Safety is predicated on the classification of the outcome, rather than on developing a deep understanding of the event and learning from an outcome of any nature. Our human brains work well in such a simplified framework. We like dichotomies. Unfortunately, the real world of organisational performance is not binary. Quantum Safety shifts the foundation of learning from reacting to specific outcomes to understanding the process.

This is not a new concept within high-performance environments. Many of the best and most successful organisations have understood and embraced the importance of the process above outcomes. The idea can be traced back to John Wooden, often referred to as the greatest coach of all time, during his career coaching basketball with the UCLA Bruins.[7] One of the many developments he made to the concept of coaching high-performance cultures was to define success as different from winning. The scoreboard or league table was not the complete story of what had occurred. This was an idea that many subsequent coaches have developed, most notably the legendary San Francisco 49ers coach, Bill Walsh. Walsh coined the term "the scoreboard will take care of itself."[8] His firm belief was that by focussing on the standard of performance, the process itself, his organisation was much more likely to achieve the success on the scoreboard they desired. It worked. In ten years, he took the worst franchise in the NFL to three Super Bowl titles.

The Lilypond Model is not driven by value judgements regarding outcomes. The purpose is always on learning for improvement. The classification of the outcome is of secondary concern. There could be significant learning from every event. Consequently, the Lilypond is multicoloured. There will be a small number of black lily pads that are of poor quality and represent poor outcomes. These need to be analysed and eradicated as much as possible. This is the Newtonian world. There are many more lily pads with a range of colours and traits that need to be explored and understood. It is the quality of the learning from the investigation of the processes that produce the lily pads that drive improvements in risk management and organisational performance. This is a theme we shall return to throughout this book.

The base of the Safety Triangle is the near miss. According to the principles of the complex, non-monochrome world of the Lilypond and the requirement for a discrete categorisation for a near misses would cease to exist. An organisation would no longer wait for an event where someone nearly got hurt, or had the potential to do so, to recognise the potential for learning. The near miss lily pad would have dissipated through the other, multicoloured pads within the Lilypond. The simple view that the near miss is the last stop before harm occurs is obsolete in our Quantum Safety understanding.

The view from above the Lilypond provides us with a more accurate and balanced perspective of organisational outcomes than previous models have encouraged (see Figure 3.4). It challenges the existing precondition of judging how bad or acceptable an outcome is before responding. Embracing this will help shape our risk management approach towards optimising learning from all events.

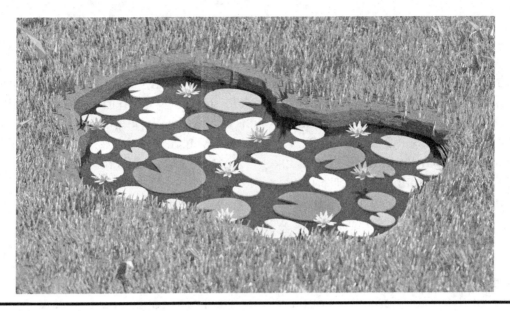

Figure 3.4   The Lilypond: a non-monochrome world.

3.2 Below the Surface of the Lilypond

3.2.2 An Intricate Ecosystem

The view from above now provides us with a more realistic and helpful understanding of our organisational performance. It helps us to answer the "what?" question. We now need to dive below the water line to begin to understand "why?". The cross-sectional view of the Lilypond provides an opportunity to understand how the wide range of organisational outcomes manifests. We are able to explore why some lily pads are black and some are beautiful. This is an intricate ecosystem, with multiple interactions, hierarchies and influences from the outside world (see Figure 3.5). It is complex and behaviours consistently change within it as creatures adapt to their immediate situation.

Each outcome begins within the system as a seed on the bed of the Lilypond. This is a natural mechanism of the workplace. The nature of the seed is not preordained; it may become a beautiful lily pad, or it could become a black one. There are no seeds that are inherently bad or inherently good. As the seed germinates and grows into its lily pad, its nature is influenced by the system. Whilst the view from above represents the frequency of each type of outcome by the lily pad, it would be more beneficial to consider each process to have its own stem which contributes and

Figure 3.5   The Lilypond: a cross-sectional view.

combines to form the view from above. This allows for learning from processes rather than grouped outcomes.

The ecosystem of the Lilypond acknowledges the complexity of our modern workplaces. Until now, we have used the SCM to infer simple attribution of cause and effect. An adverse event is viewed as a laser beam passing through defined, discrete layers of opportunity for intervention. But the growth of a lily pad is not a simple linear process. This is a significant limitation of Newtonian models being applied to the complex quantum world.

Woodward describes how

> we need to look for patterns in the behaviour of the system. We need to look for interconnections within the system rather than isolated problems ... We need to be careful when attributing cause and effect in complex adaptive systems, as we have seen it is very rarely that simple.[9]

The Lilypond Model recognises that organisational behaviours or controls are not a series of gates to pass through, but complex multi-faceted actions that require deeper investigation in order to fully understand and learn from. The nature of causation is of sufficient importance that we shall look at it in more detail specifically in Chapter 9.

3.2.3 Interactions

If we are to understand the size and colour of the lily pads, we need to understand the whole process of their growth from seed through to breaking the surface of the water. Throughout this process, complex interactions occur with the Lilypond. The seed, root and stem also have to survive encounters with the other creatures of the Lilypond, where one act could reduce the size of the pad or its colouration. These factors may help to provide some basic insight into the development of the lily pad, but it is likely that most processes are far more complex. Macroscopically, we could consider the structure of the root, how healthy it is and how it is able to withstand the currents and creatures of the Lilypond. Then microscopically, our understanding of the Lilypond could consider activity at a cellular level: the efficiency of the stomata in gaseous exchange or the process of production of glucose. It is useful to note that some of the influences affecting the growth of the lily pad are external. Light and warmth come from outside forces, which affect the outcomes just as much as biochemical interactions within the Lilypond. Political pressures, targets and seasonal demands will also have an impact on organisational performance outcomes.

This understanding has a direct implication to our idea of "systems thinking." In Safety III, Leveson explains,

> Systems Theory as used in engineering was created after World
> War II to deal with the increased complexity of the engineered
> systems being built [Weiner, 1965; Checkland, 1981, Weinberg,
> 1975] and to understand the complexity of biological systems [von
> Bertalanffy, 1969]. In these systems, separation and analysis of
> separate, interacting components (subsystems) distorts the results
> for the system as a whole because the component behaviors are
> coupled in non-obvious ways.[10]

The Charted Institute of Ergonomics and Human Factors also emphasise the importance of systems thinking:

> Serious adverse events can only be understood in terms of the
> overall socio-technical system in which the event occurred. That
> means understanding and being open to the possibility of a need
> for change in any of the components of the system.[11]

The use of terms like "engineered system" and "component" indicate a predetermined lens of analysis. This will undoubtedly be a helpful and insightful view, but potentially limited. It suggests that this methodology will investigate the Lilypond from an engineered technical point of view. To embrace the macro and micro world within the Lilypond, systems thinking should adopt the broadest possible range of views. There will be internal parts of the system at a cellular level, which, for example, would be the domain of performance psychology or constructivist language analysis, that provide insight just as much as an external structural engineered aspect of the system, which would interest an ergonomist. With this understanding of how systems thinking should be considered, it is clear that just as the development of a lily pad is more complex than the need for light, nutrients and warmth, organisational outcomes are more complex than whether or not the layers within the SCM prevent adverse events occurring. We shall revisit this idea of systems thinking in Chapter 6.

At any point, the interactions between the Lilypond and the lily stem can alter its outcome. Whilst each lily pad has its own roots, the Lilypond Model does not suggest that every individual lily pad is entirely independent of one other. They are associated. The ripples they make will impact other lily pads and their development. These are the "patterns in behaviour of the system" Woodward identifies.[9] For example, in complex organisations, we may achieve a very successful outcome for an activity, but the way in which that outcome is achieved may have a negative ripple effect on other outcomes. A great example of why this can have a significant impact on safety performance would be the work collated by Turner and his colleagues, measuring the impact of incivility in teams.[12]

A study by Porath and Erez asked participants to perform identical tasks across three experiments.[13] The task was based on using building blocks. In each experience, they varied the source and the form of rudeness enacted. In each situation, the researchers measured participants' performance, and creativity and helping behaviours were examined.

In the first experiment, the experimenter was rude to participants by belittling their reference group (students at their university) after a stooge participant turned up late for the experiment. In the second experiment, a stranger that the participants encountered on the way to the study treated participants uncivilly. In the third, the researchers asked participants to simply think about how they would react to various types of rudeness. The results were fascinating. They found that 30% fewer ideas of what to do with a block and they were 25% less creative. Participants offered simple ideas like "Build a house, build a wall, build a school." Performance drop was identical in all groups, no matter what the type and source of rudeness the participants were exposed to.

Following this, a survey of 800 businesses in 17 different industries was carried out focusing on the reactions of workers who have been on the receiving end of incivility. It is not a surprise that the results found that nearly half of the people asked (48%) intentionally reduced their productivity. More interestingly, however, the results showed that nearly the same proportion of people (47%) reduced their time spent working. It was not just productivity that suffered, but 38% people deliberately reduced the quality of their work. Efficiency dropped as 80% of people lost time worrying or replaying the act of incivility in their mind rather than working productively. A similar amount (78%) reduced their commitment to the organisation and an incredible 25% took out their frustrations of customers. Twelve per cent quit. This research shows just how important those micro interactions can be on the health of the Lilypond. The ripples and currents created cannot only impact safety performance but also the long-term viability of the organisation. This is why performance improvement should not be dominated by outcome classification and why Quantum Safety places an emphasis on understanding the process irrespective of the outcome.

For example, an individual surgical consultant may avoid using the WHO checklist preoperatively. This is ignored because his usual team complete the checklist without his involvement, ensuring that all paperwork is correct before any procedure begins. In these situations, there are micro interactions within the team that are helpful, ensuring patients are not exposed to increased risk but mask a weakness. Newtonian Safety would have to wait for an adverse event before these patterns of behaviour would be investigated. A single event could appear to be a "one-off" or bad luck as a result of the surgical consultant working out with their usual team. But there may be complex challenges around team working, communication, leadership and respect. The Lilypond Model provides a mechanism for learning to be sought irrespective of the final outcome of events.

3.2.4 Hierarchies

In any Lilypond, there are a small number of large fish who reside near the bottom of the pond. The progressively smaller fish are nearer the surface. There are also frogs, insects and crustaceans, algae and other microorganisms, all who play their part in the continuing stasis of the Lilypond. These creatures represent our workforce. Every creature has its own specialism, function and domain. This is essential. It also creates an important distinction from Newtonian Safety understanding. Newtonian Safety places responsibility for the wellbeing of the Lilypond to the largest fish, the senior leadership group. They are the most powerful creatures in the pond. But this perception increases power gradients and consequently the likelihood of authority deference within the other creatures of the pond. Authority deference is a construct that shapes a person's likelihood of intervening given their perceived place within a hierarchy. In a workplace with a pronounced sense of hierarchy, a subordinate is less likely to challenge their superior, even if they feel a decision is incorrect or dangerous. An example is the Portland Air Crash in 1978. Ten people were killed when an aircraft ran out of fuel whilst addressing a potential malfunction of the landing gear. The subsequent investigation of the incident identified several contributory factors, including the crews' inability to work together.[14] Organisations that have more mature safety cultures strive to flatten hierarchies and empower all parts of the workforce to accept responsibility for the nature and performance of the workplace. The potency of Complexity Leadership Theory,[15] shifting to the use of networks to create adaptive spaces, which can combat complexity with complexity rather than impose a desire for order, is clear (see Chapter 2). The nature of a lily pad and, therefore, safety can be created by the smallest fish near the surface by effective adaptations to their situation irrespective of what allowed the stem to develop to that point.

The Lilypond Model reinforces the importance of mutualism. For the Lilypond to thrive, the roles that all creatures play are recognised and valued. This requires the largest fish to display genuine humility and respect, so that all feel sufficiently empowered to speak up, and have the most positive impact possible within the Lilypond ecosystem. A workplace that acknowledges and celebrates the roles each creature plays, and their mutual responsibility for the health of the Lilypond, will become more reliable, sustainable and safe. It is the creatures that are smallest and nearest the surface that are most likely to be able to prevent a black lily pad from breaking the surface, by their acts or omissions. These are the work-as-done adaptations of a complex system. This reflects the more positive view of humans in a system that Safety II embraces, rather than the Newtonian perspective that humans are hazards. An effective intervention just below the surface by one of the creatures traditionally considered to be less powerful or influential can terminate the growth of a black lily pad, or transform its appearance to something more beautiful.

In such a complex ecosystem, the water can become murky. There are many interactions occurring, adaptations and growth, in an environment darkened by the sheer scale of lily pads produced above. It can be difficult for creatures, in any part of the pond, to clearly see and understand what has created their immediate environment. Equally, they may not be able to foresee the impact of their actions on other parts of the pond. It is difficult, therefore, for creatures to know what changes they can enact in order to improve the overall health of the Lilypond. This helps to understand why change within complex systems is difficult to achieve and sustain and the need to create adaptive spaces. To date, many attempts to improve safety have had negligible results. Wears and Sutcliffe cite the example of the UK Health Foundations Safer Patient Initiative, where improvement in intervention hospitals could not be directly attributed to the interventions and improvement may be explained by a "rising tide" effect.[16] Leaders and safety professionals will be well served to understand the complexity of their Lilypond in as much detail as possible before trying to change it. It would also be helpful to be able to have real data that can demonstrate that attempts to improve the state of the Lilypond have actually helped, which we shall revisit in Chapter 12.

Questions for Reflection

1. How does your organisation currently measure its safety performance?
2. How much of the Lilypond do you actually see, measure and value?

References

1. Luxhoj JT & Kauffeld K (2003). Evaluating the effect of technology insertion into the national airspace system. *The Rutgers Scholar*, 5.
2. Schein EH. (2004). *Organisational Culture and Leadership* (3rd ed.). Jossey Bass.
3. Hollnagel E. (2014). *Safety-I and Safety-II. The Past and Future of Safety Management*. CRC Press.
4. Heinrich HW. (1931). *Industrial Accident Prevention: A Scientific Approach*. McGraw-Hill.
5. Health and Safety Executive. (1999). *Reducing Error and Influencing Behaviour*. Available online at: http://www.hse.gov.uk/pubns/priced/hsg48.pdf (accessed 13 January 2021).
6. Smith AF & Plunkett E. (2019). People, systems and safety: Resilience and excellence in healthcare practice. *Anaesthesia*, 74(4): 413–548.

7. Wooden J & Jamison S. (2009). *Coach Wooden's Leadership Game Plan for Success.* McGraw-Hill.
8. Walsh B, Jamison S & Walsh C. (2009). *The Score Takes Care of Itself: My Philosophy of Leadership.* Penguin.
9. Woodward S. (2019). Moving towards a safety II approach. *Journal of Patient Safety & Risk Management,* 24(3): 96–99.
10. Leveson N. (2020). *Safety III: A Systems Approach to Safety and Resilience.* MIT.
11. Chartered Institute of Ergonomics & Human Factors. (2020). Learning from adverse events. *A White Paper.* Available online at: https://www.ergonomics.org.uk/common/Uploaded%20files/Publications/CIEHF-Learning-from-Adverse-Events.pdf (accessed 10 January 2021).
12. Turner C. (2016). Civility saves lives. Available online at: https://www.civilitysaveslives.com (accessed 13 January 2021).
13. Porath CL & Erez A. (2007). Does rudeness really matter? The effects of rudeness on task performance and helpfulness. *Academy of Management Journal,* 50(5): 1181–1197.
14. National Transportation Safety Board. (1978) *Aircraft Accident Report.* Available online at: https://www.ntsb.gov/investigations/AccidentReports/Reports/AAR7907.pdf (accessed 10 January 2021).
15. Uhl Bien M & Arena M. (2017). Complexity leadership: enabling people and organisations for adaptability. *Journal of Organisational Dynamics,* 46(1): 9–20.
16. Wears R & Sutcliffe K. (2020). *Still Not Safe.* Oxford University Press.

Chapter 4

Understanding the Lilypond Model, Organisational Safety Performance and the Performance Continuum

"We love The Lilypond Model."

"Absolutely. I was wondering if you had thought about the translational aspect? How would people use it?"

These were not the first two things they said to me, but after a connection on Twitter and some pleasantries this became the nub of the conversation. Alistair and Garin had reached out to me after my article introducing the Lilypond Model was published in a healthcare journal. Alistair is a consultant anaesthetist working in Devon, UK. People who work in healthcare tend to have a keen sense of risk and safety management. Given the risks associated with their work many anaesthetists develop an even keener interest in safety and Human Factors. Alistair is one such person. Garin is a pilot flying long haul for a global carrier. The relationship between aviation and safety is well recognised and often cited. Garin also has a keen interest in safety and risk management particularly with a view of improving the lot of frontline workers. They are also founding members of the Philosophical Breakfast Club.[1]

The Philosophical Breakfast Club is a safety-based think tank that "believes in better outcomes in risk industries. It achieves this by challenging established practice and thinking differently."[1] It was this ethos that had led

DOI: 10.4324/9781003175742-4

to Alistair and Garin contacting me. The question asked about implementation was more than reasonable. As the statistician George Box said, "all models are wrong. Some are useful."[2] We agreed that it was important that the Lilypond Model has a practical use.

Creating useful models is difficult, which is why when one is found to be useful people are reluctant to change from it. Within Complexity Science it is even more of a challenge. Miller and Page elegantly and insightfully explain how models ought to be considered in the same manner as maps.[3] There is a balance to be struck with real-life accuracy and usefulness, flexibility and precision. A good map will have all the requisite features to offer the user insights about the world in which they are navigating. If it was filled with all the information available about the area of focus, there would become too much information to be useful. This is why there are a range of maps offering analysis of the world at different layers. A road map, for example, offers a different view of the world to a topographical map. Both would be helpful depending upon the need of the user and analysis required. The various macroscopic and microscopic views provided within the Lilypond Model work in a similar manner to the multiple overlays of maps. As the conversation with Alistair and Garin evolved, it transpired that there was a map that would help the Lilypond translate into a useful tool and recognise the range of views required to understand performance in a complex organisation.

Erik Hollnagel defined safety within Safety I as "as few things as possible go wrong." In contrast, Safety II defined safety as "as many things as possible go right."[4] Leveson defined safety within Safety III as "freedom from unacceptable losses as identified by the stakeholders, but may be defined in terms of acceptable risk or as low as reasonably practicable in some fields."[5] Quantum Safety considers safety in a different frame. Philosophically, the concept is most closely aligned with Safety II, but with significant differences. Quantum Safety considers safety to be an integrated aspect of high performance.

Hollnagel challenged the orthodoxy within which we understand safety. In striving for safety excellence, it is right to analyse how most successful organisations function. High-performing teams will ensure as many things as possible go right, but one should not confuse cause and effect. Understanding the process of high performance is central to creating safety excellence and Garin had already done some great research on exactly that.

4.1 Human Factors Taxonomies

The Philosophical Breakfast Club hosts an annual conference with a range of speakers from emergency services, elite sports and safety-critical industries. It is a broad perspective to help challenge echo chambers, intellectual silos and academic bias, thus providing an opportunity for a deeper, richer understanding of the science of work. Garin undertook a thematic review of every presentation delivered at their conferences to establish the commonality arising from such a diverse group. A secondary literature review was undertaken to help supplement any themes which were less commonly or explicitly identified but were alluded to in some form. This resulted in the development of three taxonomies, which Garin kindly shared.

The taxonomies were designed to be different ways of considering Human Factors and to try to bridge the gap between academia and frontline teams. The hope, therefore, was for them to become a catalyst for change and improvement for safety-critical industries. Throughout their development it felt that there was inherent value within the analysis. The accessibility and usability of the work was less clear. The taxonomies were reformed to provide a different conceptual mechanism for them and a different language. In so doing, the relationship they had with the Lilypond Model became clear. They were the overlays of maps.

4.2 The Continuum of Human & Organisational Performance

From the three Human Factors taxonomies emerged the Continuum of Human & Organisational Performance. The Continuum was constituted of three realms: the Philosophical Realm, the Organisational Realm and the Personal Realm.

The Continuum is not designed as another model to explain performance. Neither is it a linear process, flowing left to right precisely. If analysis identifies various issues arising from within the continuum, the elements further to the left will benefit from being addressed first as those elements will continue to affect the other elements to the right of them. There is not, however, one realm which has primacy over another, nor elements within the realms. It helps move the Lilypond Model from a metaphorical world to the world of work.

4.2.1 The Philosophical Realm

One of the original aims of the research was to understand how high-performance environments are likely to be cultivated, but also why there is often a significant discrepancy between cutting-edge academic work and the lived work experience of frontline workers. The Philosophical Realm, therefore, considers the start of an academic idea and how the best work can be translated into common practice. It was this thought that energised Alistair and Garin to contact me in the first place.

The five elements within the Philosophical Realm are analytics, support, expertise, research and translation (see Figure 4.1). Analytics refers to the inception of an idea, what the need for the work undertaken is or what aspect of the world of work requires revision. If we invest in ideas that solve problems no one is seeking to address, there will be little impact on organisational performance. The work may also require support, financial or political. Well-funded research and influential advocates help advance research into reality. Expertise relates to assembling the appropriate level of capability and credibility to undertake the research, whilst being mindful of potential conflicts of interest. Some institutions will place expectations on researchers to generate work, skewing the balance between quantity and quality of outputs. With these three elements in place, the research itself can be undertaken in a manner that ensures the greatest chance of validity and relevance. The final element is translation and is an aspect that a lot of academic work finds challenging. The publication process can be slow and the articles subjected to many revisions before being accepted. The readership of academic journals is understandably mainly academics. People leading organisations or with

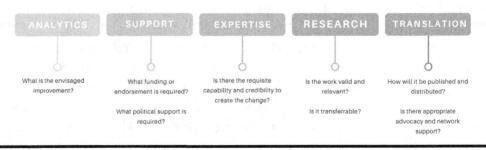

Figure 4.1 Continuum of Human & Organisational Performance: the Philosophical Realm.

a particular interest in an aspect of their work are not particularly likely to access journal articles, especially if they are behind paywalls. Even if the research is potentially transformational, getting the right people to access the research in a form in which it is accessible and relatable is a significant challenge. The result is that academic brilliance is unable to effectively be implemented and the status quo becomes further embedded.

4.2.2 *The Organisational Realm*

The Organisational Realm is where the Continuum of Human & Organisational Performance meets the Lilypond Model. The elements within this realm, as well as the Personal Realm, are facets of work that require reflection when understanding the nature and performance of the Lilypond in order to positively impact the science of work.

The five elements within the Organisational Realm are the external climate, leadership, culture, talent and working environment (see Figure 4.2). The external climate recognises that the nature of the Lilypond will be affected by factors that the organisation themselves cannot control. Legislative frameworks, political forces and professional bodies create the conditions within which the Lilypond develops. When understanding organisational performance, these external factors should be thoroughly considered. For example, in 2016 the UK changed the sentencing guidelines relating to Health and Safety Offences, Corporate Manslaughter, and Food Safety and Hygiene Offences.[6] These changes significantly increased the potential punishment for both organisations

Figure 4.2 Continuum of Human & Organisational Performance: the Organisational Realm.

and individuals in the event of a successful prosecution. In so doing, the climate changed and will have, or should have, affected organisational Lilyponds throughout the UK.

Leadership is a vast area. This book shall not offer a comprehensive literature review of all theories of leadership and how they can affect performance. Quantum Safety considers safety to be an integrated aspect of high performance. High performance is another term that is widely used but ill defined. Quantum Safety considers high performance as an environment which enables a group or team to produce sustained outcomes that are greater than the sum of its parts. There are many teams that are a collection of highly skilled professionals that achieve excellent results as a result. High performance has a greater ambition than this.

This distinction and focus on high performance can be traced back to the New View Refraction explored in Chapter 1. Behaviour-based safety, as well as a limited perspective of what systems thinking is, views the human as a rational, consistent executor of a function. This justifies a top-down order-based response to reduce the complexity observed. Safety II and Quantum Safety view humans within the systems as adaptive agents with the potential for a positive impact on organisational outcomes. It is incumbent on leadership to adopt an approach that enables this to be positively channelled and utilised.

Quantum Safety does not advocate one sole approach to leadership. It is important that organisations adopt a leadership approach which they feel is most conducive for success. Broadly, to enable greater adaptive spaces and move away from command and control, leaders who are more compassionate and enabling will find the change quicker and more effectively. Also, the Lilypond Model identifies the importance of mutualism. The power gradients that leaders create and sustain should be reflected upon as to their appropriateness and the impact they have elsewhere in the Lilypond.

Culture is at the centre of the Continuum. This is apt. That being so, we shall explore culture in much more detail in Chapter 7. Central to understanding culture is the role fear plays within the decisions made and how organisations react to things that have gone wrong.

The fourth element in the Organisational Realm is talent. Talent is not an often-used parlance in many high-risk industries. In sectors that attribute most value to frontline staff, such as entertainment and elite sports, we do tend to use this vernacular. The implicit respect and inferred sense of mutualism by adopting the term are deliberate and important. Broadly, when considering the talent within the organisation we are thinking about the creatures of the Lilypond. What specialisms do they bring to help ensure the Lilypond is both healthy and productive. Talent identification and retention, or recruitment and human resources if the reader prefers, are integral to creating a high-performance environment.

Bill Walsh, legendary San Francisco 49ers coach, took a typically insightful view of this aspect. If he observed a player routinely make a mistake, Walsh would not reprimand the player, but rather his coach. Walsh rationalised that it was the coach who must've failed in his duties creating the conditions for the player not to succeed.[7] Similarly, if an organisation wishes to address a team that is poorly performing, or has a poor micro culture, they would be well served to consider first who made the decisions in regard to talent acquisition in the first place.

The final part of the Organisational Realm is the working environment. Environment is a term that can become conflated with the idea of culture. Indeed, it is understandable to relate the two concepts. Within the Continuum, working environment is concerned with the existence of a high challenge – high support environment which is foundational for high performance. Within this the micro-interactions between people are contained as well as the general ambience of the organisation. The importance of Psychological Safety would also be an integral factor within the working environment. This allows us to consider what it means to be a creature within the Lilypond and whether they are likely to be able to thrive.

4.2.3 The Personal Realm

The final part of the Continuum is the Personal Realm. This now moves the perspective from that of the overall Lilypond and on to individual creatures and their actions. The five elements within this final realm are wellbeing, learning, equipment and resources, professional actions, adaptive skills (see Figure 4.3).

Wellbeing considers a similar aspect of work to the working environment, but from the individual perspective. What is the impact upon the working conditions created by the organisational environment for individuals? What is the consequence of working in the organisation for those working at all levels? There are a wide range of individual considerations of merit within

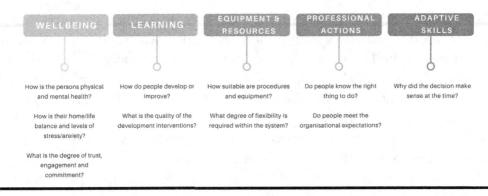

Figure 4.3   Continuum of Human & Organisational Performance: Personal Realm.

this element. Interpersonal factors such a trust, engagement and commitment as well as internal factors such as the balance between challenge and threat situations, level of arousal or stress and sense of purpose, all merit reflection.

High-performance organisations continually develop. This includes a focus on the continual development of individual talent. Work-based training is often focussed on compliance and competency. There is nothing inherently wrong with this for a learning and development department. The quality of the development opportunity is something that is more variable as methodologies used, or resources identified for this, struggle to maintain parity with best educational practices. Content which is of limited value with little or ineffective feedback offered is not congruent to an expectation of high performance.

In order for people to be expected to perform to the best of their ability they need to be provided with the right tools for the job. The element of equipment and resources considers more than the physical tools. The role user centred design of all equipment and systems should be championed within any high-performance organisation.

Professional actions address the implementation of work. The actions and decisions taken being commensurate with the training and competency of individuals, and also in line with company expectations and safe systems. This is also a traditional view of the role of people at work outlined in previous chapters. In this element, people know the right thing to do and are in a position to do it.

In the rich, interconnected world of complex systems there are many decisions or situations where goals are conflicted or the concept of the right choice ambiguous. Adaptations will frequently occur throughout the Lilypond. The relationship between professional actions and adaptive behaviours in complex systems is an important relationship to understand, especially in terms of safety performance. This shall be explored more comprehensively in Chapter 6.

4.3 Using the Continuum of Human & Organisational Performance

The Continuum provides ten specific elements for consideration to help understand the Lilypond, as well as five important elements that provide a map to understand the academic evolution of an idea. The conversations with Garin and Alistair evolved from taxonomies to continuums and from explanations to diagnostics. The Continuum can be used as an indicative tool to help understand performance within the Lilypond and hence map out a strategic vision for improvement.

In order to demonstrate this analysis, we shall consider maternity safety. In particular the maternity services at Telford and Shrewsbury Hospital NHS Trust.[8] Donna Ockenden chaired an independent review of the services upon the request of the Secretary of State for Health following concerns raised by bereaved parents. The initial review was tasked to consider 23 tragic cases. The final report considered 250.

Before further progress is made, a few points require absolute clarity. The Ockenden Report is the only source of information used and some parts of the analysis may not be as complete as organisations can do themselves with access to more complete information. Also, this is not a comprehensive diagnosis of the NHS Trust that is the subject of the report. The human tragedy that instigated this investigation is not be minimised or lost.

The following are a series of statements from the Ockenden Report and suggestions as to how the Continuum of Human & Organisational Performance can be used to help place the observations within a framework in order to understand their Lilypond.

> One of the most disappointing and deeply worrying themes that has emerged is the reported lack of kindness and compassion from some members of the maternity team at the Trust.

This would suggest that the micro-interactions within certain teams or at certain times were poor. The working environment created within the Organisational Realm was not acceptable. There would be consequential questions, therefore, about the leadership approaches adopted and also potentially around the acquisition of talent.

> Inappropriate language had been used at times causing distress. There have been cases where women were blamed for their loss and this further compounded their grief. There have also been cases where women and their families raised concerns about their care and were dismissed or not listened to at all.
> There is also evidence that when concerns were escalated they were not then acted upon appropriately or escalated further to the appropriate level. This may indicate a lack of multidisciplinary communication and collaboration and/or senior clinical supervision, both of which are key to providing safe care.

Again, this would indicate concerns about the functioning of teams within high-emotion, high-pressure situations and the lack of the appropriate level of support for people to excel within the working environment. This would also be influenced by a culture with an unhealthy relationship with blame, fear and accountability. Individually, there would be concerns around professional actions and potentially learning and development as concerns were not listened to or acted upon; however, this should be expected behaviour within such a culture.

> The review team found evidence in a number of cases of repeated attempts at vaginal delivery with forceps, sometimes using excessive force; all with traumatic consequences. There was clear evidence that the operating obstetricians were not following established local or national guidelines for safe operative delivery.

This is an incredibly upsetting observation that provides a range of possible diagnoses. There is a clear divergence between the work that was carried out and the safe systems of work established by the appropriate professional bodies. This should bring into question an individual's professional actions. The quality of the individuals' learning and ongoing personal development should also be considered if obstetricians were failing to follow such guidelines on a more consistent basis.

> The review team have the clear impression that there was a culture within The Shrewsbury and Telford Hospital NHS Trust to keep caesarean section rates low, because this was perceived as the essence of good maternity care in the unit.

The direct reference to culture would encourage people understandably to focus on culture within the Continuum. A culture that misunderstands or applies the misguided analysis of the surface of the Lilypond indicates leadership approaches that attempt to apply for top-down order in order to meet goals or expectations created by the external climate.

> We also found several examples of lack of senior involvement from the consultant anaesthetists on call. Even in periods of high workload, there was limited support by the consultant anaesthetist responsible for the delivery suite out-of-hours.
> Limited consultant anaesthetist representation in incident investigation and multidisciplinary team meetings after significant incidents.

In tandem these statements indicate concerns specifically in the micro culture of the anaesthetic department. The Continuum could be applied specifically to this department in the same manner it has been to the whole Trust so far. The acquisition of talent specifically within this department would warrant more scrutiny in the same manner Bill Walsh would challenge his coaches. This accruement of talent within the anaesthetic department may have allowed their micro culture to be fostered on leadership approaches that are neither compassionate nor enabling. Consequently, individuals' working conditions would be unlikely to be at the requisite standard to enable them to succeed consistently. Furthermore, it would question how aligned the department was with the overall Trust in terms of influential people's degree of engagement and motivation.

This simplified diagnostic process will not have accurately identified all aspects that the Ockenden Report did. It does help identify some of the issues that consistently appeared to be a concern within their Lilypond. The multiple overlays that the Continuum is able to offer help to simultaneously simplify the messy reality of the modern workplace as well as provide a bridge from the metaphorical world of the Lilypond Model.

The entire Continuum does, however, help form a more comprehensive understanding of the high-performance process. The Philosophical Realm can also provide insight and routes to improvement. A few weeks before the Ockenden Report was published there was a Healthcare Select Committee at the Houses of Parliament that focused on the topic of maternity safety and in particular the role that litigation plays.[9] I was asked to work with one of the expert witness's testimony using some of my work on safety culture. The hearing centred on the recognition of the fact that other countries, in particular Sweden and New Zealand, appeared to have far better outcomes in regards to maternity safety. They also have very different legal systems in relation to harmed families. The burden of proof required for harmed families, in order to receive compensation, is set much lower in the other countries where harmed families have to demonstrate that the care provided was substandard. In the UK, people have to prove harm beyond a reasonable doubt.

The high standard required for the burden of proof in the UK creates an adversarial system which automatically places organisations, and consequentially the clinicians within them, in a defensive, threatening environment. The work, therefore, in the Philosophical Realm, identifying up-to-date thinking, requires translation into practice. This will have a significant impact on the external climate for such organisations, which will ultimately change the performance of the Lilypond and the various creatures working within it.

Organisations will want to be able to apply the Lilypond Model to their own workplace. To do so they will be able to use the various overlays that the Continuum of Human & Organisational Performance enables.

Question for Reflection

What external factors affect the climate in which your organisation develops its risk management approach?

References

1. www.thephilsophicalbreakfastclub.org.uk
2. Box GEP. (1979). Robustness in the strategy of scientific model building. In Launer RL & Wilkinson GN (eds.), *Robustness in Statistics*. Academic Press. pp. 201–236.

3. Miller JH & Page SE. (2007). *Complex Adaptive Systems: An Introduction to Computational Models of Social Life.* Princeton University Press.

4. Hollnagel E. (2014). *Safety-I and Safety-II. The Past and Future of Safety Management.* CRC Press.

5. Leveson N. (2020). *Safety III: A Systems Approach to Safety and Resilience.* MIT Press.

6. Health and Safety Offences, Corporate Manslaughter and Food Safety and Hygiene Offences Definitive Guideline. (2016). [online] available at: https://www.sentencingcouncil.org.uk/wp-content/uploads/Health-and-Safety-Corporate-Manslaughter-Food-Safety-and-Hygiene-definitive-guideline-Web.pdf [Accessed 15.02.21].

7. Walsh B, Jamison S & Walsh C. (2009). *The Score Takes Care of Itself: My Philosophy of Leadership.* Penguin.

8. Ockenden, D. (2020). Emerging findings and recommendations from the independent review of maternity services at the Shrewsbury and Telford Hospital NHS Trust. [online] available at: https://www.ockendenmaternityreview.org.uk/wp-content/uploads/2020/12/ockenden-report.pdf [Accessed 15.02.21].

9. Healthcare Select Committee. (2020). Formal hearing (oral evidence session): Safety of maternity services in England. [online] available at: https://committees.parliament.uk/event/2533/formal-meeting-oral-evidence-session/ [Accessed 15.02.21].

Chapter 5

A Different School of Quantum Safety: Moving into the Experimental World

There are two schools of physics. There is a theoretical approach and an experimental. Theoretical physics uses abstractions and models to explain and rationalise things that happen. Experimental physics uses tools to probe the things that we wish to understand.[1] A theoretical physicist can develop an idea without the need for any empirical data to prove it. That is the job of experimental physicists.

For example, String Theory is one of the most popular modern advances in quantum physics. It proposes that matter is not made up of particles but rather tiny strings.[2] These are so small as to appear as particles to the observer. Many physicists consider String Theory to be the best hope of creating a unified theory of everything. This is despite there being a few conflicts that the theory, as it stands, is unable to address. The main conflict is the idea of inflation, or as most people would understand it – the big bang. String Theory is not tested empirically. Some argue it's untestable.[3] Notwithstanding those challenges, the attraction of the theory remains.

Quantum Safety does not afford itself such luxuries. Both the theoretical and the experimental schools are accommodated. The theory of understanding organisational safety as an integrated aspect of high performance within the complex world of the Lilypond requires testing. The Continuum of Human & Organisational Performance moves the concept from the

DOI: 10.4324/9781003175742-5

philosophical to the real world. It can also be developed into a tool to allow organisations to begin to understand their Lilypond.

There are tools that already exist that profess to perform exactly this task. Safety culture or climate assessments are readily available. The two of the most widely used approaches are based upon the Bradley Curve[4] and Hudson's Organisational Maturity Model.[5] The Bradley Curve was developed by DuPont and depicts a convex line of injury rates culminating in the ultimate goal of zero injuries. Behind this, four differing levels of safety maturity are proposed, namely reactive, dependent, independent and interdependent, that change as the injury rates progress. The Hudson Organisational Maturity Model shares many of the same foundational principles as the Bradley Curve. Hudson's Model offers a ladder with five categories of safety maturity ranging from the pathological level 1 to generative level 5.

The appeal of such models is understandable. Despite various attempts by consulting firms to repurpose and repackage these, the value of the insights they provide is less clear. It is not clear how easy or possible it is to mount the scale from pathological to generative.[6] Indeed it is not always clear whether the organisational goal is to aspire to become generative. Whilst many of the characteristics of a level 5 safety culture would be congruous with the principles outlined within Quantum Safety, some are not. Furthermore, these tools are all based developed from Newtonian Safety. Whilst that remains a valid perspective to adopt, it will fail to provide as rich an understanding of organisational performance that Quantum Safety provides.

The accuracy of insights offered by using such a maturity ladder is not proven. Indeed, research conducted across multiple sectors "suggests that maturity models are widely used by organisations eager to gain some insight into their safety culture. Much of this activity might be characterised as 'experimenting' with maturity models."[7] I have facilitated many such experimenting sessions with organisations in safety-critical industries. These have been conducted with varying degrees of rigour. The results have been much less varied. One format, which I shall call group 1, involved inviting groups to paw through the descriptors of various characteristics envisaged at each level. The group would then discuss and agree an aggregate position based on this. Alternatively, I have asked other groups, which I shall helpfully call group 2, to instinctively provide a value between 1 and 10 for their organisational safety culture, with 10 being safety utopia. I have done this with hundreds of groups over the years with either format. The first group would, after much vexation and analysis, almost always state that they were somewhere between level 3 and level 4, between calculative and proactive. With the second method the group would typically offer scores between 6 and 7. The consistent logic behind these values was that they were pretty good, not amazing, could be better but could be much worse. The groups usually had a good idea of what much worse looked like. There was always another group that was identified as much worse. The other group was usually contractors, clients, management or competitors depending on the nature of the group I was working with. They were almost universally scored as level 2, or 4 out of 10, depending on the method adopted. The area for real improvement was always elsewhere.

This is all perfectly reasonable and an acceptable way to begin to get groups to consider their safety culture. It is not remotely surprising. In the 1980s, there was a study carried out that analysed children's judgement of their own and their classmate's academic ability.[8] The study found that children's judgement of their own ability reduced as they got older. Presumably this process ran parallel to their experience of the world telling them that they were pretty good, not amazing, could be better, but could be much worse. The scores they provided for their colleagues were always lower, in precisely the same manner my groups considered their competitors. Improvement was really for others. Distilling a culture to a place on a curve or a rung on a ladder, therefore, may ultimately offer the same degree of insight as posing the question to a group of six-year-olds.

The solution is to move away from a snapshot overview of safety climate and towards a longitudinal analysis of organisational performance. The Continuum of Human & Organisational Performance provides the ability to do precisely this and move from the theoretical world of the Lilypond into the experimental.

To understand how an organisation is represented along the Continuum each element will in turn be considered. This will provide a profile and help identify areas for development. Each element consists of five self-reflection questions which will provide an opportunity to analyse the approach to performance at both macro and micro levels. Whilst such tools are always subject to a degree of subjectivity, the potential for cross-sectional analysis from differing teams and departments can make the process more scientifically valid than asking for people to score themselves out of 10.

The first part of the Continuum, the Philosophical Realm, will not be configured into part of the indicative tool. A comprehensive analysis of the academic sphere would not offer significant insights to organisations. This is not to disregard entirely the Philosophical Realm. The example from the previous chapter of maternity care within the NHS highlights the significant potential improvement for risk management if the best research is translated quickly into practice. Organisations would therefore be well served to reflect on this realm before proceeding with their own indicative process, or upon completion to begin to identify new approaches to aid improvement.

5.1 The Organisational Realm

Tables 5.1–5.10 allow organisations to reflect and consider more deeply the structural underpinning that creates the environment for organisational performance. It will begin by reflecting on the external climate that will

Table 5.1 Organisational Realm: External Climate

Element: External climate	Strongly disagree	Disagree	Neutral	Agree	Strongly agree	Value
The legal and regulatory framework allows us to fully pursue our objectives	1	2	3	4	5	
The legal and regulatory framework improves the ability to manage risk	1	2	3	4	5	
The safety culture within the sector is congruent with our objectives	1	2	3	4	5	
The employment market enables us to access appropriate talent	1	2	3	4	5	
Clients and contract-awarding bodies fully support our risk management approach	1	2	3	4	5	
Total score (max 25)						

Table 5.2   Organisational Realm: Leadership

Element: Leadership	Strongly disagree	Disagree	Neutral	Agree	Strongly agree	Value
The leadership approach is compassionate and respectful	1	2	3	4	5	
Roles and authority are clear and consistently adhered to	1	2	3	4	5	
The leadership demonstrate high trust behaviours	1	2	3	4	5	
Leadership create and communicate a clear strategic direction	1	2	3	4	5	
Leadership are highly aware of the reality of work in the organisation	1	2	3	4	5	
Total score (max 25)						

influence the organisational Lilypond. The previous example regarding Maternity Safety within the NHS (see Chapter 4) shows the importance of this, as well as the role that the Philosophical Realm has in shaping this. Each table will allow a specific element within the Performance Continuum to be analysed and provide a score out of 25. This can then be mapped to form a profile upon conclusion (see Figure 5.1).

5.2 The Personal Realm

The same approach as the Organisational Realm is undertaken within the Personal Realm. The focus now shifts from how the organisation functions to a consideration as to how the individual is able to perform within the conditions created by the organisation. The creatures within the Lilypond are now in our thoughts rather than the nature of the pond in which they operate.

Table 5.3   Organisational Realm: Culture

Element: Culture	Strongly disagree	Disagree	Neutral	Agree	Strongly agree	Value
Culture is not built upon blame and fear	1	2	3	4	5	
People are able to report concerns or issues safely	1	2	3	4	5	
The culture is based on a concept of growth and improvement	1	2	3	4	5	
All people feel they will be treated fairly and with respect	1	2	3	4	5	
Organisational reaction is not dictated by the outcome of events	1	2	3	4	5	
Total score (max 25)						

Table 5.4   Organisational Realm: Talent

Element: Talent	Strongly disagree	Disagree	Neutral	Agree	Strongly agree	Value
People are treated with real inclusivity and equality	1	2	3	4	5	
Staff turnover is low	1	2	3	4	5	
Applications for role vacancies is high	1	2	3	4	5	
People are given a lot of time and resources to develop themselves	1	2	3	4	5	
People will speak well of their experience when leaving the organisation	1	2	3	4	5	
Total score (max 25)						

Table 5.5 Organisational Realm: Working Environment

Element: Working environment	Strongly disagree	Disagree	Neutral	Agree	Strongly agree	Value
People feel enabled to challenge others, including more senior people, when required	1	2	3	4	5	
People welcome challenges from their colleagues at all levels	1	2	3	4	5	
All people feel supported in order to meet expectations	1	2	3	4	5	
The organisation creates the optimal conditions for people to succeed	1	2	3	4	5	
Total score (max 25)						

Table 5.6 Personal Realm: Well-Being

Element: Well-being	Strongly disagree	Disagree	Neutral	Agree	Strongly agree	Value
People feel that their work is valuable and valued	1	2	3	4	5	
Work-induced stress is not problematic	1	2	3	4	5	
People are appropriately remunerated	1	2	3	4	5	
People are happy in their work	1	2	3	4	5	
People are able to work safely (physical, occupational and emotionally)	1	2	3	4	5	
Total score (max 25)						

Table 5.7 Personal Realm: Learning

Element: Learning	Strongly disagree	Disagree	Neutral	Agree	Strongly agree	Value
Training is an opportunity to stretch and develop people	1	2	3	4	5	
Feedback offered is helpful and developmental	1	2	3	4	5	
Learning is based on worked reality rather than theory	1	2	3	4	5	
Individuals are involved in their development and learning	1	2	3	4	5	
Training and development is valued throughout the organisation	1	2	3	4	5	
Total score (max 25)						

5.3 Creating your Continuum Profile

The data generated from fully considering the elements of both the Organisational and Personal Realms can be easily turned into a visual indicator of how the organisation correlates to the principles of high performance (see Figure 5.1). It is important to recognise that this profile is not a result in itself in the same way that organisations have previously placed themselves on curves or ladders. Rather, it is a means to understand more deeply the process of performance and help identify areas that warrant attention and redress.

Organisations could gain valuable insights by allowing different teams or divisions to explore the Continuum separately. The differences in the profiles created by different groups may indicate behaviours within sub-cultures across the organisation. They could also help identify a differing view of the reality of what life is like in the Lilypond between the larger fish operating near the bottom and the other creatures. Effective leaders should be curious

Table 5.8 Personal Realm: Equipment and Resources

Element: Equipment and resources	Strongly disagree	Disagree	Neutral	Agree	Strongly agree	Value
Systems are designed to help people perform to their best	1	2	3	4	5	
Resources provided are reliable and well maintained	1	2	3	4	5	
Issues and concerns are appropriately addressed	1	2	3	4	5	
Equipment is designed/sourced to help people to perform to their best	1	2	3	4	5	
Processes and procedures are suitable for high-pressure and emergency situations	1	2	3	4	5	
Total score (max 25)						

and compassionate in trying to understand the differing perspectives this can help identify.

This allows us to use the Continuum of Human & Organisational Performance to reflect and gain an indication of how the organisation can improve performance. It translates the Lilypond from the theoretical to the experimental. Before further insights of how our approach to risk management can be understood from the complex world of the Lilypond, there are some elements in particular that require greater consideration. Culture, in particular the concept of the Just Culture, which is often perceived to be the standard-bearer for creating safety cultural excellence, will be critically analysed in Chapter 7. Before that, greater consideration of the final elements of the Performance Continuum is required to understand their dynamic relationship within the complex systems of the modern workplace.

Table 5.9   Personal Realm: Professional Actions

Element: Professional actions	Strongly disagree	Disagree	Neutral	Agree	Strongly agree	Value
People are clear about their role and expectations of performance	1	2	3	4	5	
People are clear when and where to get assistance	1	2	3	4	5	
Expectations are clear for all tasks	1	2	3	4	5	
Assistance is provided promptly when required	1	2	3	4	5	
All people meet competency requirements set by internal and external bodies	1	2	3	4	5	
Total score (max 25)						

Table 5.10   Personal Realm: Adaptive Skills

Element: Adaptive skills	Strongly disagree	Disagree	Neutral	Agree	Strongly agree	Value
People consistently act with high integrity and trust	1	2	3	4	5	
Adaptations are not judged by the outcome	1	2	3	4	5	
All adaptations are valued and learned	1	2	3	4	5	
People embrace accountability in emergency and high-pressure situations	1	2	3	4	5	
Adaptations improve organisational outcomes	1	2	3	4	5	
Total score (max 25)						

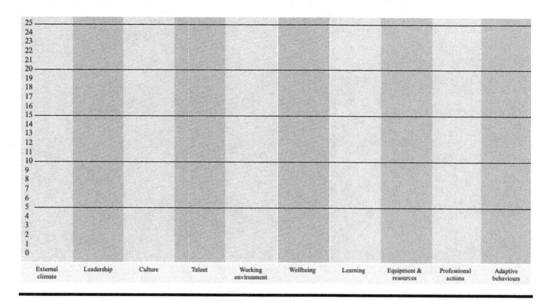

Figure 5.1   Continuum of Human and Organisational Performance Profile.

Questions for Reflection

Develop your Continuum of Human & Organisational Performance profile (see Figure 5.1). Explore differences of perspectives between individuals, teams and departments.

References

1. Rovelli C. (2016). *Seven Brief Lessons on Physics*. Penguin Books.
2. Zweibach B. (2004). *A First Course in String Theory*. Cambridge University Press.
3. Cartwright N & Frigg R. (2007). String theory under scrutiny. *Physics World*, 20(9): 14.
4. Jasiulewicz-Kaczmarek, M, Szwedzka, K & Szczuka, M. (2015). Behaviour based intervention for occupational safety: Case study. *Precedia Manufacturing*, 3: 4876–4883. [online] Available at: https://doi.org/10.1016/j.promfg.2015.07.615 [Accessed 02.03.21].
5. Hudson P. (2001). Aviation safety culture. *Safeskies*, 1: 23.
6. Hale AR. (2006). Method in your madness: System in your safety. Delft University of Technology, 15th September. [online] Available at: https://www.researchgate.net/publication/27351879_Method_in_your_madness_ system_in_ your_safety [Accessed 02.03.21].
7. Filho, APG & Waterson P. (2018). Maturity models and safety culture: A critical review. *Safety Science*, 105: 195–211. [Online] Available at: https://doi.org/10.1016/j.ssci.2018.02.017 [Accessed 02.03.21].
8. Stipek DJ & Tannatt LM. (1984). Children's judgments of their own and their peers' academic competence. *Journal of Educational Psychology*, 76:1.

Chapter 6

The Human Performance Foxtrot

Quantum Safety is a markedly different frame to other emerging views on safety, as an integrated aspect of a high-performance organisation. It offers a new conceptual model with which to explore the modern complex workplace and move away from historic linear models. The Continuum of Human & Organisational Performance can be used as an indicator to help organisations understand their Lilypond Model and bridge the gap between theory and practice. Quantum Safety also offers more comprehensive revisions around ideas of causation (see Chapter 9) and culture (see Chapter 7) within the complex, high-performance environment. Before these concepts can be developed, the final part of the Continuum of Human & Organisational Performance requires greater analysis. The interrelationships between professional actions, adaptive behaviours and also equipment and resources would benefit from the clarity that further consideration.

These three elements could be considered to come under the purview of Human Factors and Ergonomics (HFE) to varying degrees. Precisely where the boundaries of HFE expertise reside, however, is not clear. It is irrefutable that HFE is an important and powerful vehicle for improving safety and quality across high-risk industries. As our understanding of the science of work and thinking around systems has evolved, the scope of HFE has also grown. The Chartered Institute of Ergonomics & Human Factors (CIEHF) claim five knowledge areas: anatomy and physiology, psychology, people and systems, work environment and methods and tools. Each knowledge area subsists of multiple individual specialist domains

DOI: 10.4324/9781003175742-6

including physiotherapy, process analysis, ethics, statistics, and behaviours and attitudes. In total HFE claim specialist knowledge in 67 disciplines. These are *all* important facets of understanding and improving the workplace and would be relevant throughout the Continuum of Human & Organisational Performance, not only the final three elements of equipment and resources, professional actions and adaptive behaviours. Whether one body can, or should, lay claim to such a supercontinent of knowledge is less clear.

When learning from adverse events, CIEHF advocates the principle of adopting a systems-based approach, in line with Leveson's Safety III methodology.[1] Such an approach is predicated by an "understanding and being open to the possibility of a need for change in any of the components of the system."[2] Systems thinking centres "on the dynamic interaction, synchronization, and integration of people, processes, and technology."[3] As the Lilypond Model explains, systems thinking requires a more holistic view with multiple perspectives. Effectively integrating people into a process is one important mindset. Whilst this approach is essential to helping create an optimal and safe working environment, in safety-critical industries adopting such a single focus will not create the improvement in organisational performance alone. The confusion of what HFE may or may not be is incredibly unhelpful. Human Factors should not be considered a solo sport.

6.1 Systems Soliloquy

Hollnagel argues that safety is not a property of a system, rather it is a "characteristic of how the system performs."[4] Systems will have other characteristics such as productivity, efficiency and quality. People operate within the system whilst simultaneously being shaped by these system characteristics. Safety is not an isolated process. Quantum Safety recognises this, which is why it considers safety as an integrated aspect of organisational performance, in which there are permanent trade-offs between all system characteristics.

There are situations and environments where these trade-offs prioritise safety. The protocols introduced for donning and doffing PPE when undertaking an aerosol-generating procedure (AGP) of a COVID-19 positive patient would be one such scenario. In order to safeguard people at work when entering and exiting areas that were known to be at high risk of infection, rigorous validated procedures were installed within all hospitals. Within these measures, visual cues were supplied to provide exact templates of a sequence of actions to don and doff as well as additional fail-safe measures. Whilst there will be varying iterations of systems in differing localities, there is no scope for adaptive behaviour within the specific protocols introduced so that the task is ultra-safe. So far, so very Safety III.

6.2 Systems Dance Partner

It is somewhat tautological to explain that a global pandemic is a highly unusual working environment. In such extreme circumstances, an approach solely predicated on systems is entirely appropriate. In most environments the approach to safety requires greater nuance and flexibility. There also needs to be an understanding of the nature and necessity of adaptive behaviours, which is the final element within the Continuum of Human & Organisational Performance.

Adaptive behaviours are identified by a range of labels within safety and human factors. Terms such as violations, variation and deviance are often cited.[2,5] The concept of different types of work, such as work-as-imagined, work-as-prescribed, work-as-done and work-as-disclosed, is also a helpful framework for conceptualising adaptive behaviours.[6]

Typically, adaptations are considered to be detrimental to optimal safety outcomes. Dekker describes them as "the seeds for failure."[7] These normal behaviours include workarounds, improvisations and adaptations, but may also just be normal work behaviours routinely undertaken to get the job done.[8] The conventional solution is to engineer a resilient system that reduces and restricts adaptations. Whilst good system design is necessary for all safety-critical environments, Quantum Safety considers the conventional view to be overly simplistic when behaviours within complex adaptive systems are fully considered.

6.3 Partners on the Dance Floor

Before the dynamic relationship between adaptive behaviours and systems thinking can be developed, the framework in which they interact needs to be considered. We need to understand the dance floor on which they will perform. The excellent model by Vincent and Amalberti[9] provides the most suitable platform (see Figure 6.1).

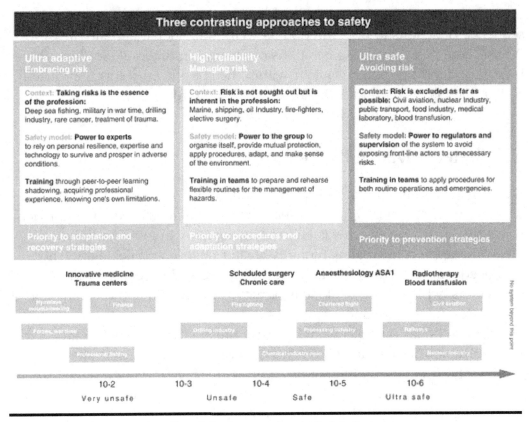

Figure 6.1   Vincent & Amalberti "3 Approaches to Safety".

Vincent and Amalberti developed Three Approaches to Risk Management. This helped explain a world where there was not a one-size-fits-all approach to managing risk. Different industries, environments and circumstances would require different approaches. These approaches would have differing advantages and limitations with differing trade-offs "between the benefits of adaptability and the benefits of control."[9]

The previous example of donning and doffing PPE in COVID-19-positive areas is easily applied to this model and sits neatly in the ultra-safe third. In that situation the best approach was entirely dependent on making the system resilient with no scope for safe adaptive behaviours. The systemic dynamics, or how the work is being done, will require more flexibility as other parts of the model become relevant. The relationship between fundamentally design-orientated approaches that create systemic resilience, such as Safety III, and the value of adaptive behaviours, such as Safety II, becomes more important to creating an environment where safe optimal outcomes occur.

6.4 Dancing the Foxtrot

The foxtrot is a smooth, progressive dance characterised by long, continuous flowing movements across the dance floor. Quantum Safety considers this to be a more helpful conceptual framework to envisage the relationship between adaptive behaviours and systemic resilience. This is a significant shift from adaptations being considered seeds of failure. Created dichotomies such as these with value judgements placed upon discrete actions don't exist within the complexity of reality. The world is neither binary, nor linear, and our understanding of systemic properties would benefit from embracing this. That is not to say that adaptations or everyday workarounds can't become seeds of failure. In such circumstances, a comprehensive review of the system and the properties it creates with work-as-done would be crucial for improving future outcomes. As a default mindset, however, it is limiting.

Hollnagel takes a different view from Dekker and the "seeds of failure" approach to adaptations, instead suggesting that "humans are seen as a resource necessary for system flexibility and resilience."[10] In Safety III, Leveson typically critiques Hollnagel's approach observing that Hollnagel

> uses the term "humans" a lot, but put into context, it appears that he is talking almost solely about low-level workers and operators in simple workplaces. There are lots of humans in our systems; humans design systems, manage them, certify them, maintain them, as well as operate them. But most of his assertions seem only to apply to operators and seem to omit the sophisticated human factors research and human-centered design in engineered, complex systems today.[1]

There is much to ponder with these three competing views aside of the inadvertent implicit message that low-level workers and operators are less capable of sophisticated decisions than researchers, designers and engineers. The Lilypond Model clearly identifies the importance of all the creatures within the system, each with differing and important skill sets required to generate the outcomes of the organisation. Those outcomes will be, partly at least, produced as a result of adaptive behaviour throughout the Lilypond, which is why understanding more completely the relationship between certain elements within the Continuum of Human & Organisational Performance is crucial. In so doing, Quantum Safety recognises there is merit in both points made by Hollnagel and Leveson without falling into a limited perspective as a result of the refraction of New Views of Safety.

The degree of adaptive behaviours within systems is surprising. Even a process which would be considered to be simple can display considerable variation in performance. There has been some great research by Matt Scanlon and his colleagues who have researched complexity within healthcare settings. Their study was part of a broader AHRQ-funded study (1 R01 HS013610).[11] They looked at processes which were thought to easily be able to provide a simple, linear flow chart outlining the correct process of drug administration to a patient. Over 100 hours of medication administration process were observed by human-factors-trained researchers, resulting in a 44-page document, detailing multiple long, complex flow charts of the process. Simple, linear models of workplace processes are likely to be highly flawed. This adds weight to the notion that a system can simultaneously be considered to be simple or complicated as well as complex in the same way that light can be both a wave and a particle. To ignore adaptive behaviours, or to think a system can be designed to apply sufficient control and order, is misguided. Adaptive behaviours will be present, it is their effect we need to understand.

To explore this idea further, we need to go around the world. More accurately we shall learn from what occurs in the high-risk environment during round-the-world yacht racing.

The vessel in question has a mainsail. This is the big sail at the back which is attached to the mast. The boom is a large piece of metal attached horizontally to the mast which can swivel from side to side. On larger boats the boom can weigh several tonnes, so should it swing unexpectedly or in a direction that is not desired it can kill members of the crew instantly. There is also a mainsheet. This is a line that controls the mainsail. This can potentially whip across the boat when the sail flips from one side to another if there is any slack within the mainsheet which is not ideal if you happen to be in the way of that whip. To slow down the movement of the boom, a line appropriately called a preventer is attached to the boom.

During the Round the World Race, a standard operating procedure was bought in to say that two lines were to be attached to run as preventers to create a failsafe should one of the lines snap. This meant, however, that when the crew were turning, the process was lengthened because they had more lines to detach. The process was already incredibly high risk and this new system required crew to be in the "danger zone" for longer on the low side of the vessel where risks of going overboard or being struck from recoiling lines were readily present. Consequently, many crews chose to either not attach the second preventer at all, or to do so after the turn had been completed. They adapted to varying degrees, dependant on crew experience and interpretation of the risk, so that they could turn as quickly and as safely as possible.

This scenario is not the inverse of the PPE scenario outlined previously. There are still a number of systems adhered to by the skipper and their crew. These create a foundational level of safety. Again, we can observe the misguided desire to create order and ignoring the Law of Requisite Complexity.[12] The highly skilled, experienced professionals are subsequently able to adapt using this foundational level of safety provided by the system and create a more flexible and appropriate solution. It is worthy of note that research within the fire service conducted in order to understand how decisions are made in emergency situations has identified similar behavioural and systemic constructs[13] to which we shall return to in Chapter 11.

The science of understanding the adaptive decision-making in high-pressure situations falls under the umbrella of cognitive engineering.[14] The vernacular of both the design-orientated resilience engineering that focuses on making systems rather than individuals resilient and actions under pressure focus of cognitive engineering is understandable and logical. These labels, however, also perpetuate a paradigm of linearity and dichotomy. Effective approaches for understanding human performance in safety-critical industries require greater scope for flexibility as well as multidisciplinary collaboration, rather than a predominant approach of decision-making or design. The example of the Round the World crew demonstrates the success that this dynamic, flexible combination can have.

An organisation will be able to develop an effective approach to understanding human performance by understanding where the organisation, or specific environments, are on Vincent and Amalberti's three-stage dance floor. There also needs to be careful thought into the choreography to ensure the most appropriate mixture of both cognitive engineering and resilience engineering is required.

6.5 Understanding the Dance

The Human Performance Foxtrot can now smoothly progress across the dance floor. There is no predetermined direction or value judgement on either part. The objective is to now understand what insights it offers about the nature of the work and how to create conditions for optimal, safe outcomes (see Figure 6.2).

No industry sector provides a homogenous work environment. The nature of the work and the risks that a sector entails will be vastly different depending on the context in which the work is being done. It would be reasonable, for example in healthcare, to expect far fewer adaptive behaviours within radiology as there would be in psychiatry or accident and emergency departments. In maritime, the race crew we discussed earlier would be much more adaptive than a large shipping container vessel.

There are occasions where adaptations can be excluded by design. There are occasions where adaptations can enhance outcomes. There will also be occasions where adaptive behaviours can help create a condition of safety but mask an underlying systemic failing. The packaging of drugs would provide a good example of such dynamics.

Here we have two drugs (see Figure 6.3). The vial with the pink label is fentanyl. This is a painkiller frequently used as part of a general anaesthetic in operating theatres. At this dosage, if administered to an adult, most people would come to no harm and feel highly relaxed. The second vial with the white and yellow label is suxamethonium. Suxamethonium is a muscle relaxant also widely used as part of an anaesthetic. The vial shown would render the patient unable to breath within a minute. Both vials, with clear liquids and similar packaging, would be easy to mix up. The consequences of such a mistake could be grave.

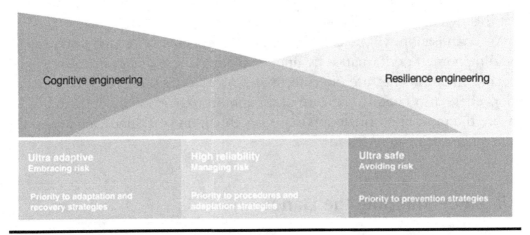

Figure 6.2 The dynamic relationship between adaptive behaviours and resilience engineering within different risk profile environments.

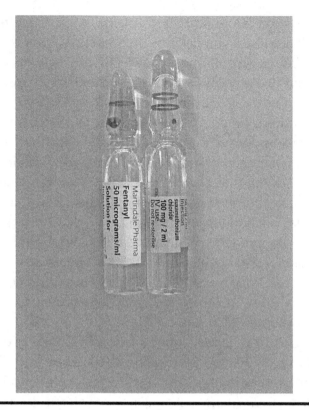

Figure 6.3   Vials of Fentanyl (left) and Suxamethonium (right).

In such a situation, optimal safe outcomes for patients are reliant on the ability of anaesthetists to add resilience to the system by circumnavigating the potential to mix up these drugs. It is, however, the system that has a weakness and needs redress. Adaptive behaviours are not, therefore, inherently seeds of failure. Neither are they a substitute for the design of robust systems that are fit for purpose. It should not be a surprise that complex adaptive systems require a mindset that goes beyond a simple, linear "adopt a systems approach."[1,2,5]

6.6 Why We Need to Embrace Our Partner

The purist "safety by design" approach has limitations. Even in industries considered to be consistently ultra-safe with a high requirement of systemic or engineering solutions to improve safety, to do so at the expense of completely ignoring their adaptive behaviour dance partner, can prove to be actual seeds of failure. In 2015, Germanwings flight 9525 crashed killing

150 people after the co-pilot committed suicide. A protocol introduced post 9/11 required pilots to lock the door to their cockpit. This is the system that enabled the co-pilot to commit mass murder. This tragic event suggests that not only were there weaknesses within the systems and equipment part of the Personal Realm of the Continuum but also concerns about personal well-being, which would not be addressed by a narrow systems view. It should be noted that Leveson does also refer to this crash within Safety III explaining that there are times that "restraining performance variation is exactly the right thing to do" adding that events such as the Germanwings crash "are much less likely than the need to prevent bad guys. These are the types of decisions that must be made in engineering."[1]

A systems-based approach will always be very important. The relationship between systems approaches and adaptive behaviours needs to be more fully considered within each context and environment. At times adaptations will be unhelpful. At others they may be necessary, sometimes they are desirable for optimal outcomes.

Exploring the text from large inquests following major events demonstrates the need to a greater understanding of the Human Performance Foxtrot. Simple interpretations of complex events do little to help understand events and improve performance. A major terror attack is a perfect example of a complex system. The goals of all stakeholders are unclear, optimal decisions are highly conflicted and there will be a high number of people reacting in the best possible way with imperfect information in a highly volatile situation. The Kerslake Report was an independent review into the preparedness for, and emergency response to, the 2017 Manchester Arena bombing following an Ariana Grande concert.[15] During the event a heroic paramedic had self-deployed to the emergency, and even after being told by a police officer that there was a suicide bomber entered the "hot zone." The heroic actions of zero and first responders were commented upon during the final report.

During the coroner's inquest into the 2017 London Bridge terrorist attack which killed eight people, the paramedic response drew criticism for following protocols for such emergencies and not entering a "hot zone" until told it was safe to do so.[16] The adaptive behaviours observed during the Manchester Arena attack were raised in a manner to highlight the professional actions of the paramedics at London Bridge as insufficient. In two highly comparable, complex and risky situations, the decision to follow the system or not was considered to be optimal and not optimal. As is often the case with a Newtonian Safety mindset, the decisions were judged retrospectively skewed by value judgement placed on the outcome. The people involved in those tragic events, who displayed incredible bravery, deserve a better and useful framework to work within.

Analysis will require a more respectful, collaborative and nuanced approach to developing approaches that truly understand human performance in order to improve organisational outcomes: one that eschews simple, linear answers and embraces complexity; one based within the non-monochrome world of the Lilypond. The final three elements of the Performance Continuum consequently can be considered as separate blocks, but also as an interrelated, dynamic manifestation of a system. It is a flowing progression of a dance.

It is time to engineer less. Put the music on and listen.

Questions for Reflection

1. What is the current mindset regarding adaptive behaviours?
2. Where would your organisation operate within the three-stage dance floor?
3. Are risk management systems created to enable people to succeed?
4. Which activities present different requirements for adaptive behaviours?

References

1. Leveson N. (2020). *Safety III: A Systems Approach to Safety and Resilience*. MIT.
2. Chartered Institute of Ergonomics and Human Factors. (2020) Learning from adverse events. [online] Available at: https://www.ergonomics.org.uk/common/Uploaded%20files/Publications/CIEHF-Learning-from-Adverse-Events.pdf [Accessed 03.03.21].
3. Trbovich P. (2014). Five ways to incorporate systems thinking into healthcare organizations. [online] Available at: https://pdfs.semanticscholar.org/6599/7e90979d780be5e9e6f5ae8bcb7d5f010c1b.pdf [Accessed 04.03.21].
4. Hollnagel E & Woods D. (2006). Resilience engineering. [online] Available at: https://www.researchgate.net/profile/David_Woods11/publication/265074845_Epilogue_Resilience_Engineering_Precepts/links/546b62c70cf2397f7831bdfc/Epilogue-Resilience-Engineering-Precepts.pdf [Accessed 06.03.21].
5. HSG48: Reducing error and influencing behaviour. Health & Safety Executive [online] Available at: https://www.hse.gov.uk/pubns/priced/hsg48.pdf [Accessed 21.02.21].
6. Shorrock S. (2016). The varieties of human work. [online] Available at: https://humanisticsystems.com/2016/12/05/the-varieties-of-human-work/ [Accessed 11.10.20].

7. Dekker S. (2011). *Drift into Failure: From Hunting Broken Components to Understanding Complex Systems*. Ashgate.
8. Shorrock S, Leonhardt J, Licu T & Peters C. (2014). Systems thinking for safety: Ten principles. *A White Paper*. [online] Available at: https://www.skybrary.aero/bookshelf/books/2882.pdf [Accessed 13.03.21].
9. Vincent C & Amelberti R. (2016). *Safer Healthcare*. Springer.
10. Hollnagel E. (2014). *Safety-I and Safety-II. The Past and Future of Safety Management*. CRC Press.
11. Holden RJ, Joy Rivera-Rodriguez A, Faye H, Scanlon MC & Karsh B-T. (2013) Automation and adaptation: Nurses' problem-solving behavior following the implementation of bar coded medication administration technology. *Journal of Cognition, Technology and Work*, 1;15(3): 283–296.
12. Boisot M & Mckelvey B. (2011). Complexity and organization-environment relations: Revisiting Ashby's law of requisite variety. In Peter Allen, Steve Maguire & Bill McKelvey (eds.), *The Sage Handbook of Complexity and Management*. Sage Publications. pp. 279–298.
13. Wilkinson B, Cohen-Hatton SR & Honey RC. (2019). Decision-making in multi-agency groups at simulated major incident emergencies: In situ analysis of adherence to UK doctrine. *Journal of Contingencies and Crisis Management*, 27(4). pp. 1–11.
14. Endsley MR, Hoffman R, Kaber D & Roth E. (2007). Cognitive engineering and decision making: An overview and future course. *Journal of Cognitive Engineering and Decision Making*, 1(1, Spring). pp. 1–21.
15. Kerslake B. (2018). *Kerslake Report: An Independent Review into the Preparedness for, and Emergency Response to, the Manchester Arena Attack on 22nd May, 2017*. [online] Available at: https://www.jesip.org.uk/uploads/media/Documents%20Products/Kerslake_Report_Manchester_Are.pdf [Accessed 06.03.21].
16. Mark Lucraft QC. (2018). *Coroners Inquest into London Bridge and Borough Market Terror Attack on 3 June 2017*. [online] Available at: https://londonbridgeinquests.independent.gov.uk [Accessed 06.03.21].

Chapter 7

The Just Culture: Why It Isn't Just and How It Could Be

In its own right culture is a vast element of understanding organisational performance. It is a widely used term that frequently presents itself when safety-related matters are reviewed. In recent years, reviews, investigations and inquiries have frequently cited organisational culture within their findings. In 2016, an independent inquiry into the climate and culture of the world-class programme within British Cycling found there to be a "culture of fear and bullying."[1] Following two fatal air crashes of the 737 Max aircraft, a congressional investigation found Boeing to have a "culture of concealment."[2] In 2013, the Members of Parliament found "a blame culture had developed in Whitehall over recent years, with ministers and civil servants unwilling to take responsibility for failures, such as the West Coast Mainline franchise debacle or in defence procurement and immigration."[3] In 2020, former Health Secretary Jeremy Hunt MP said that the world-renowned Great Ormand Street Hospital in London may have "profound cultural problems"[4] after several issues around patient safety and whistle-blowers were published. In safety-critical industries, the term culture is often prefixed with the notion of just.

James Reason proposed the idea of a Just Culture. He defined Just Culture in his seminal work *Managing the Risks of Organisational Accidents* as "an atmosphere of trust in which people are encouraged, even rewarded, for providing essential safety-related information, but in which they are also clear about where the line must be drawn between acceptable and unacceptable behaviour."[5] The move towards a Just Culture was proposed as an

DOI: 10.4324/9781003175742-7

alternative to the prevalent culture of blame and fear. Since then, many high-risk industries, including aviation, healthcare and rail, have used this concept to define and shape cultural change. Within his work, Reason did not only propose a Just Culture. Rather a Just Culture was a foundational principle to eradicate the behaviours or inactions resultant of fear and expectation of blame. A Just Culture preceded a Reporting Culture. If an employee expects that they would be treated fairly in the event of an accident or mistake, they would be more likely to report the issues present. This would help perpetuate a Learning Culture where an organisation, in possession of relevant safety concerns, could take appropriate action which, in turn, creates an organisational safety culture.

Any attempts to move away from blame-based approaches to safety, or ones where fear is a consistent characteristic within decision-making towards a culture that is fairer, are surely steps in the right direction. The vision set out by James Reason is as brilliant as it is important. There are, however, problems with James Reason's Just Culture. Firstly, it has proved astonishingly difficult to achieve. Secondly, and possibly the reason why it has proven difficult to achieve, is that Just Culture as presented currently is not particularly just. It is time to review the idea of Just Culture, its philosophical framework and ways in which we can work to enable and sustain the cultural change desired.

7.1 Leaving Blame

Initially efforts were made in many industries to move towards a culture of zero blame; however, James Reason powerfully argued that whilst this was a step in the right direction it failed to address those individuals

> who wilfully (and often repeatedly) engaged in dangerous behaviours that most observers would recognise as being likely to increase the risk of a bad outcome. Second, it did not properly address the crucial business of distinguishing between culpable and non-culpable unsafe acts.[6]

High-performance organisations have a healthy relationship with accountability. A Just Culture was designed to enable organisations to improve as a result of this relationship with accountability.

The objective of establishing a Just Culture is not a new one. In 2001, with an aim of putting quality at the forefront of healthcare and changing the way medical mistakes were addressed, the UK government released a joint declaration alongside the GMC, the Royal College of Surgeons and the Academy of Royal Medical Colleges. A commitment to quality, a quest for excellence, made seven pledges that had been agreed between government and healthcare professionals.[7] These included the recognition that

> in a service as large and complex as the NHS things will some-
> times go wrong. Without lessening the commitment to safety and
> public accountability of services, the signatories agree to recognise
> honest failure should not be responded to by blame and retribu-
> tion, but by learning and a drive to reduce risk for future patients.[7]

Despite this, the cultural change experienced by frontline workers has not materialised. In 2018, a survey of over 150,000 people working in UK's health service found that 95% were sometimes, or often, fearful of making mistakes.[8] It would be difficult to argue that the NHS is currently operating a Just Culture even after talking about it for nearly 20 years. Failing to create a true Just Culture is not an issue solely of the UK healthcare systems. Edwards studied 270 hospitals in the USA and found that

> the evidence suggests that, in aggregate, US hospitals have per-
> fected a system for casting blame among both physicians and
> nurses. In such a hostile environment, self-reporting would be
> career suicide. So whatever the effect of just culture, it clearly has
> not fulfilled its promise to eliminate the culture of blame and gross
> underreporting of opportunities for improvement, which continue
> to hamper progress in patient safety.[9]

This inertia is not a phenomenon peculiar to healthcare. In a similar manner to other terms, such as Safety II, the understanding of Just Culture is often variable. This was ably demonstrated by a director of health and safety and self-proclaimed behavioural safety expert within a major construction company, who via a series of company roadshows ensured everyone understood that the last thing they wanted to create was a Just Culture. Apparently, to this company a Just Culture was a toxic and dangerous culture where people walked past safety concerns, shrugged and rationalised the situation as "just what happens here." Equally, other companies have introduced a Just Culture policy only to find it weaponised and people get "just cultured."

Aviation is often considered to be more successful in achieving this culture change. Unfortunately, the evidence does not support the idea that aviation has a true Just Culture. The recognition that Boeing had a "culture of concealment" which led to the safety issues surrounding the 737 Max aircraft has been identified. Additionally, "in a survey of 53 European aviation organisations most organisations admitted to still having to work on the 'no-blame' aspects of a just culture in relation to mistakes made."[10] There is general acceptance that there is a healthy reporting culture within aviation where pilots consistently report errors and mistakes. This is something other industries often wish to imitate, but to conflate it with being a Just Culture is inaccurate. As a group of pilots shared with me, given all decisions within the cockpit are already recorded it may be easier for pilots to offer such important candour.

It appears that whilst to err is human, so too is our propensity to blame. Our idea of what a Just Culture is and how we create one requires a complete overhaul.

7.2 Revisiting the Idea of Justice

The intellectual journey from a blame to a no-blame culture and beyond to a Just Culture is important and valuable. It is, however, important to understand the context in which those decisions were made. Our current, modern workplaces and understanding of organisational safety are markedly different to those around which the early Just Culture models were based. The current climate of both safety and Just Culture requires further examination.

Eurocontrol is a European-based, civil military organisation dedicated to supporting European aviation. As the network manager, Eurocontrol strives to maximise safety performance across aviation, working with over 200 airlines and over 3,000 pilots worldwide. In 2020 they published a Just Culture manifesto. The aim of this manifesto was to "articulate a vision of Just Culture" globally across all industrial sectors and to "provide a framework for other people to advance this vision of Just Culture."[11] The manifesto is constituted of five commitments, which are:

■ Ensure freedom to work, speak up and report without fear.
■ Support people involved in incidents and accidents.

- Don't accept unacceptable behaviour.
- Take a systems perspective.
- Design systems that make it easy to do the right thing.

The manifesto has been widely supported and hundreds of people have signed up to these principles. Quantum Safety should be considered compatible or complementary to all of the five commitments within this manifesto. That is not to say, however, that the manifesto should be considered to be the optimal vision for Just Culture across all industrial sectors.

The first principle is not surprising or controversial. It closely relates to the original work of James Reason regarding the creation of an atmosphere of trust and combatting the toxic effects of a culture based on fear. A more modern lexicon for this, widely used when understanding the science of work, is Psychological Safety.[12] Amy Edmondson at Harvard University first constructed the term "Team Psychological Safety" within the workplace.

Despite its label, Psychological Safety is not something developed within or for safety professionals. It is a broader concept concerning organisational performance and behaviours. Edmondson defines Psychological Safety as "a shared belief held by members of a team that the team is safe for interpersonal risk taking."[12] Google undertook a project designed to understand what was required to build a high-performing team, named Project Aristotle. The most important factor it found in team performance was Psychological Safety. This does not only mean the ability to report defects or concerns, but the ability to report those concerns freely without fear is helped by Psychological Safety within the workplace.

The second principle is also reasonable. It is not concerned with the emotional well-being of anyone involved within an investigation process. The move towards a more humanistic approach is certainly important in creating a Just Culture.

In its strictest sense, the third principle is a paradox. It is impossible to accept the unacceptable. The adjoining guidance explains that "gross negligence and wilful misconduct are very rare, but cannot be tolerated."[11] Quite. Exactly how this advances understanding or implementation of a Just Culture is not clear.

The final two principles are closely linked focused as they are on the system. Analysis with a wider view of the overall system is integral to Quantum Safety which is why the Lilypond Model provides a crucial new conceptual frame compared to linear Newtonian models. The caveat with these principles is the breadth in which systems thinking is understood. With due consideration to the Human Performance Foxtrot, it would be injudicious to prejudice analysis to a default-design-based solution. Design of a system will always be very important, but not exclusively so. Also, whilst these principles are valid in line with a mature approach to application of Human Factors within an organisation to improve safety performance, they are not themselves foundational principles of a Just Culture. The Eurocontrol manifesto as a whole has merit, but in terms of Quantum Safety is best considered to be incomplete.

Sidney Dekker, as part of Safety Differently, has proposed an alternative approach to Just Culture based on restoration. Dekker explains that a Restorative Just Culture "aims to repair trust and relationships damaged after an incident. It allows all parties to discuss how they have been affected, and collaboratively decide what should be done to repair the harm."[13] Dekker argues that this is a more humanistic approach to Just Culture than Reason's, which Dekker considers to be retributive. He argues,

> A retributive just culture can turn into a blunt HR or managerial instrument to get rid of people. It plays out between "offender" and employer—excluding voices of first victims, colleagues, community. A retributive just culture is linked with hiding incidents and an unwillingness to report and learn. The more powerful people are in an organization, the more 'just' they find their retributive just culture. A retributive response doesn't identify systemic contributions to the incident, thus inviting repetition.[13]

The humanistic perspective echoes the second principle within the Eurocontrol manifesto.

The Restorative Just Culture approach has gained some traction in sectors such as healthcare. A more humanistic methodology has merit for sure. Some of Dekker's criticisms of the classical approach, which he dubs Retributive, require further consideration. Reason very clearly explained the desire for establishing an "atmosphere of trust." Any poorly understood or implemented tool or system can become counter to its true intention. This does not mean that the concept itself is flawed. Whilst there is little evidence of successful creation of Just Cultures, to conclude they are linked "with hiding incidents and an unwillingness to report and learn"[13] appears like a wilful attempt to misappropriate Reason's concept of Just Culture. Finally, the suggestion that "systemic contributions to the incident"[13] are not identified is at best inaccurate. There are many iterations and derivations of Reason's

Just Culture, but they consistently question the provision of safe systems of work. There is a significant difference between inaccuracy and absence. In a similar manner, Reason's Just Culture may be conceptually flawed which explains why it is so rarely established, but that does not mean that the criticism Dekker outlines is proportionate, accurate or reasonable.

The vision of a Restorative Just Culture also requires consideration as to whether the changes offered will make the cultural progress to help create the optimally safe productive environment. Repairing the trust and relationships damaged after an incident is important and not debatable. The emphasis placed on this, however, does create a concern. There is a tacit acceptance with this definition that reactions to adverse events will negatively affect trust and relationships, making this concept essentially a reactive one. Dekker's Restorative Just Culture sometimes adopts the sobriquet of a Just & Learning Culture. It is a claim which is difficult to substantiate in the evidence provided. On Dekker's Restorative Just Culture Checklist, which is offered as a "better way" to do Just Culture, there are five areas of consideration broken down into 22 sub-questions. Learning is mentioned once. This is the 22nd consideration; "organisational learning – explored and addressed systemic causes of harm. Yes. No."[13] Such prioritisation is simply incongruent with high-performance environments. A Restorative Just Culture indicates at important elements that previous Just Culture concepts missed, but its reactionary foundation and concerning prioritisation of improvement, or lack of it, render this approach equally as flawed and limited as Reason's.

7.3 Just Culture for the Modern Complex Workplace

Given the limitations of the existing Just Culture model and the debatable progress made over the past 20 years in creating it, this author proposes a new approach to Just Culture. This approach will have a new definition of what we ought to consider a Just Culture, a manifesto clearly identifying what principles need to be consistently applied as well as a proposed algorithm to help operationalise it.

Reason defined a Just Culture to be "a culture in which front-line operators and others are not punished for actions, omissions or decisions taken by them which are commensurate with their experience and training, but where gross negligence, wilful violations and destructive acts are not tolerated."[4] This is the definition that Eurocontrol based its manifesto upon. As we have seen Dekker's Restorative Just Culture "aims to repair trust and relationships damaged after an incident."[13] Quantum Safety offers a new vision. Just Culture within Quantum Safety is one that creates an environment to learn, grow, heal and excel. This is a significantly broader and more holistic vision predicated on high performance rather than failure avoidance.

A Just Culture that enables both individuals and organisations to learn, grow, heal and excel is developed upon four principles. This is the Quantum Safety manifesto for a Just Culture.

- Safety I & Safety II
- Learn not blame
- Systems thinking
- Civility and respect

7.3.1 Safety I and Safety II

The Just Culture proposed in 1997 was developed within the Newtonian Safety frame of Safety I. A Just Culture proposes that by adopting an approach that is transparent and fair, workplace staff will gain greater trust in the organisational system. Classically, this approach focuses solely on how people respond to adverse events due to their Safety I origin. This is a presumption that has been tacitly accepted thus far. There is a clear paradox in these two aspects of the current Just Culture approach. It should be reasonably expected that all adverse events only constitute a small percentage of organisational outcomes, most likely less than 5%, because for any organisation to function it must be able to produce a far higher number of successful outcomes than unsuccessful ones. It is implausible to have a system that is transparent and fair, that creates trust, if it ignores the 95% of organisational outcomes that are not adverse events, yet this is precisely the classical Just Culture construct. Furthermore, Dekker's restorative Just Culture is designed only for Newtonian Safety thinking and has no way of being applied to other events. A Just Culture that integrates Safety I and Safety II must recognise more than 5% of organisational outcomes for it to be truly just. The entirety of the surface of the Lilypond is part of a Just Culture, rather than having a special process for a select few outcomes.

7.3.2 Learn Not Blame

One of Dekker's criticisms of Reason's Just Culture is that it perpetuates a blame culture. This was clearly not the aim of Reason's work, the contrary in fact. Reason tries to apportion blame appropriately. Blaming fairly is a fundamentally different approach to truly being fair, however. The implications on safety and workplace culture are significant. By identifying the impact that the focus on liability has on potential investigations, Dekker identified an important issue requiring redress. The balance of the solution offered though is not conducive to creating the environment desired.

Reason argued that a Just Culture would lead to a Reporting Culture which would, in turn, instil a Learning Culture. Quantum Safety agrees with the importance of creating a learning culture, but the evidence to date suggests the linear, sequential model offered by Reason doesn't work. Quantum Safety doesn't recognise a chain of events from a Just Culture to a Learning Culture. Instead, Quantum Safety considers that ideas of Just and Learning cultures are entangled.[14] The approach within Quantum Safety is to prioritise, for all events, learning rather than liability, and in so doing will perpetuate trust to a far greater extent.

Advocates of Reason's Just Culture model will argue that it does provide an opportunity for learning. There is scope to identify mitigating factors, although what constitutes a mitigating factor isn't specified, and the role the protocols and processes may have played within any adverse event. Reason's model poses some important questions following an adverse event, but not necessarily in the right order. The priority, and focus, of the model is calculating the degree of individual liability.

Prioritising learning does not in any way minimise the importance of personal accountability. In high-performance environments personal accountability is a healthy, positive and important facet. This is why expecting all people to work within their professional actions is an individual element of the Continuum of Human & Organisational Performance. Dekker's Restorative Just Culture considers accountability to be forward looking, asking who is obligated to redress the hurt. Healing the hurt is part of the revised concept of Just Culture and these questions are valuable. To minimise ownership of actions ignores the reality of the regulatory and legal framework that are especially important in safety-critical industries. Failing to recognise the external climate and how it affects organisational culture displays a limited understanding of the science of work.

7.3.3 Systems Thinking

In a complex socio-technical system, behaviours and decisions need to be understood within the context that pertains to them. Indeed, we should ask at every stage of investigation, "Why did that decision make sense at the time?"[15] This is localised rationality. Analysing individual decisions without having first analysed the culture within which they were taken would be at best prejudicial to any learning. Context, cultural norms and complexity have no role within the classical Just Culture model apart from an all-encompassing final consideration of mitigating circumstances. This consideration of mitigating circumstances would also rely on the people applying the process being willing and able to apply such analysis. If their leadership instinct is to blame, then the opportunity to consider mitigating factors will be lost. Well-intentioned practitioners may lack the depth of understanding to identify and learn from such mitigating factors.

For example, the first question in a model based on Reason's work is often "Was there intention to cause harm?" The second question covers ill health and substance abuse. The priority of these two initial facets is not congruent with a culture interested in learning. For example, following an adverse event in a hospital, the first questions we ask someone who is most likely a committed, diligent, caring healthcare professional (who is likely to be experiencing a degree of trauma, shame, guilt and concern as a result of the event) are whether they are actually a psychopath and if they have taken drugs or are in any other way lacking the faculties to do their job. It is perhaps not surprising that the process is not felt to be just or focused on learning, as the 2018 BMA survey for doctors in training shows.[8]

A Just Culture approach based on apportioning liability after an adverse event also fails to recognise many other opportunities from which complex systems can, and should, learn. As with most Newtonian orthodoxy, the outcomes dictate the process. The Lilypond Model allows a more nuanced view identifying that there are many micro-interactions within complex systems. These micro-interactions are invaluable opportunities to learn and improve as Woodward identifies, "we need to look for patterns in the behaviour of the system. We need to look for interconnections within the system rather than isolated problems."[16] A Just Culture approach that fails to take into account these patterns in a complex system will miss these opportunities for valuable learning.

These micro-interactions may represent repeated and systemic weaknesses which are valuable opportunities to learn. If we adopt an outcome-based methodology, where we only examine adverse events, we can miss these weaknesses until harm has occurred. Systemic weaknesses might be masked by adaptations by colleagues or other parts of the system, which ultimately create an acceptable outcome or safe event as identified within the Human Performance Foxtrot (see Chapter 6). No learning occurs because in our outcome-based world, there is no need to try and learn when something goes right. Using the Lilypond Model, the lily pad may be of any colour, or nature of outcome; however, it is the stem, the process that enabled its growth, where the focus of investigation and understanding should be. Our current approach is generally one of reaction to only the black lily pads which are the adverse events, and the investigative process looks at their stems in isolation. A true Just Culture should, therefore, not be driven by a value judgement of an outcome, but instead should provide a consistent methodology to learn from any behaviours and actions within a complex system.

7.3.4 Civility and Respect

There are many ways in which the traditional approach to Just Culture could be considered to be lacking in respect. Firstly, to ignore an overwhelming majority of outcomes only to react when we fail is understandable due to our Newtonian Safety legacy but not respectful to those at work. To initiate a procedure designed to instil confidence by asking about their criminality and potential substance abuse is also misguided. A culture that enables people and the organisation to learn, grow, heal and excel recognises that with the rarest of exceptions people work with good intention. Our analysis should be founded on that principle. This demonstrates a basis of respect and a commitment to compassionate leadership.[17] The contrast to the first question asked within the traditional model discussed is stark. It is important that we recognise that the majority of people within a high-risk environment are making decisions where there isn't always an obvious good or bad option.

In Chapter 3, the Lilypond identified the importance of micro-interactions on performance. The importance of civility throughout all operations should also be incorporated into our approach to Just Culture. This will also help people to heal and ensure the process is positive and healthy for all concerned.

7.4 A New Model

A new approach is needed in order to create an environment that enables people to learn, grow, heal and excel. This approach has been designed with the four parts of the manifesto to be consistently applied and offer a route to turn theory into practice (see Figure 7.1). The new model has three main components.

Firstly, this new model is based wholly on a presumption of good intention to recognise the importance of civility and respect. Within a true Just Culture, in a complex, high-risk industry that is both compassionate and respectful, the first consideration ought not to be one of individual negligence. Furthermore, this foundation enables the full spectrum of organisational outcomes to be considered rather than solely focusing on adverse events so we can apply it to the whole of the Lilypond Model. Now a Just Culture approach can learn from excellence as easily as it can learn from failure.

The next main component is analysis within the cultural context. It no longer considers the stem of the lily pad in isolation but takes into account the entire ecosystem within which it grew. If we accept a presumption of good intention, we need to understand why the decision or actions made sense at that time and the context in which they were taken[15] local rationality. Most Just Culture approaches are predicated on a rule-based approach. These become quasi-human-resource tools and concern themselves with work-as-imagined. This shift in focus allows us to instead prioritise an understanding of work-as-done. This also enables the approach to integrate Appreciative Inquiry within a Just Culture. Appreciative Inquiry is an approach adopted to address what is working well and seeks to build on this, instead of a more traditional focus on problems and weaknesses. The Appreciative Inquiry "approach doesn't pretend there are no real or challenging problems, but it asks you to look at them and redefine them in a way that generates a number of positive possibilities."[18] The respectful learning approach within Appreciative Inquiry naturally synergises within this revised idea of Just Culture and allows people to heal and grow.

The final component of the model encompasses personal factors, which is where the classical model operates. The main revision is the order of questions, with the concern regarding intention becoming the final question. Having completed a more comprehensive analysis of the decisions within the context of a complex system, the organisation would be finally in a position to consider that the individual displayed poor intention or negligence, and subsequently apportion liability, and the consequences of that, appropriately.

The model is designed to identify opportunities for learning throughout. There may be some behaviours that are rare or unique. These events may

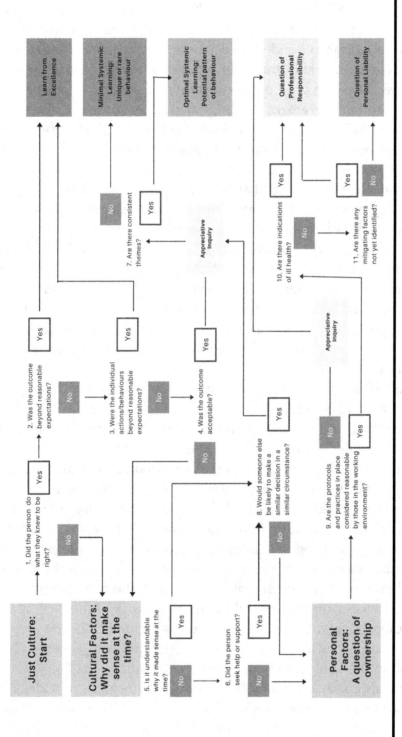

Figure 7.1 Just Culture within a complex system.

offer valuable insights into emergency or unusual event, but given their rarity it is less likely to provide valuable cultural learning that can be applied throughout a department, site or organisation. Also, this new model allows patterns of behaviour to be identified. These are the patterns of behaviour or micro-interactions within the complex system that may indicate a potential weakness. These would be a good source of potential learning for the organisation and improvement using QI methodology (see Chapter 12).

This proposed Just Culture model does not revert to an approach of no blame. Personal responsibility is considered and analysed. If individual actions have not met the standard that would reasonably be expected of someone with their professional skill and expertise, this would be identified and they would have to accept appropriate responsibility for the event. Individual consequences would be taken in line with HR policies and procedures. Likewise, individuals whose actions have fallen significantly below what would reasonably be expected of someone with their professional skill and expertise are recognised. This could result in contact relevant regulatory bodies, suspension of staff, and referral to police and disciplinary processes. This is an approach focused on creating excellence; it is not a free pass for people within the system to eschew accountability or ownership.

The need for movement towards a Just Culture has been highlighted since the 1990s and attempts have been made to achieve progress. But during this time, little real change has been felt by those working on the front line, as has been demonstrated by repeated surveys of frontline workers. A culture of blame and fear remains pervasive throughout high-risk industries, where staff perceive apportioning liability to be a central focus.

The inertia is not due to a lack of desire to create a Just Culture. Progress is restricted by the suitability of the models provided for use. Simplistic, linear-based ideas of processes minimise understanding of human behaviours and adaptations within our complex systems. Opportunities to learn are missed due to an approach that is dictated by the nature of the outcome rather than focusing on understanding the process. And the lack of presumption of good intention in all staff creates an implicit blame mechanism, especially as decisions and behaviours are often not comprehensively considered within the context in which they were made.

This new approach, with its four underlying principles, provides a route to excellence in safety-critical industries. This will help organisations to raise performance and create a culture where learning is prized over liability, where compassionate leadership can become embedded and where staff are presumed to be trying to do their best in the initial stages of any investigation into their working practices. The aim of a Just Culture originally stated by James Reason, to create an atmosphere of trust, may then become established.

Questions for Reflection

1. To what extent does the perception of fear or blame affect people's attitudes towards risk management in your organisation?
2. From what events do we learn?

References

1. Phelps A, Kelly J, Lancaster S, Mehrzad J & Panter A. (2017). *Report of the Independent Review Panel into the Climate and Culture of the World Class Programme in British Cycling.* [online] Available at: https://www.sportsthink-tank.com/uploads/cycling-independent-review-7.pdf [Accessed 14.03.21].
2. Committee of Transport and Infrastructure. (2020). Final Committee Report. The design, development & certification of the Boeing 737 Max. [Online] Available at: https://transportation.house.gov/imo/media/doc/2020.09.15 %20FINAL%20737%20MAX%20Report%20for%20Public%20Release.pdf [Accessed 15.03.21].
3. House of Commons Public Administration Select Committee. (2014). More complaints please! The Stationary Office Ltd. [online] Available at: https://publications.parliament.uk/pa/cm201314/cmselect/cmpubadm/229/229.pdf [Accessed 20/03/21].
4. Hunt J. (2020). Why the blame culture within the NHS needs to change: and as quickly as possible. *The Independent.* [online] Available at: https://www.independent.co.uk/voices/nhs-great-ormond-street-hospital-jasmine-hughes-safety-b1760980.html [Accessed 19.03.21].
5. Reason J. (1997) *Managing the Risks of Organisational Accidents.* Ashgate.
6. Reason J. (2004). *Aviation.* [online] Available at: https://www.skybrary.aero/bookshelf/books/233.pdf [Accessed 10.03.21].
7. Wise J. (2001). UK government and doctors agree to end "blame culture." *BMJ*, 323(7303): 9.
8. Wise J. (2018). Survey of UK doctors' highlights blame culture within the NHS. *BMJ*, 362: k4001.
9. Edwards MT. (2018) An assessment of the impact of just culture on quality and safety in U.S Hospitals. *American Journal of Medical Quality*, 33(5): 502–508.
10. Aksellson R, Koornneef F, Stewart S & Ward M. (2009). *Resilience Safety Culture in Aviation.* [online] Available at: https://pdfs.semanticscholar.org/9601/aafd44ad79cb03935d562ea18e2180526f01.pdf [Accessed 10.03.21].

11. Shorrock, S (2020) Just culture manifesto. Eurocontrol. [online] Available at: https://www.skybrary.aero/bookshelf/books/5880.pdf [Accessed 21.03.21].
12. Edmondson AC. (2019) *The Fearless Organisation: Creating Psychological Safety on the Workplace for Learning, Innovation and Growth.* Wiley.
13. Dekker S (2018) Restorative Just culture checklist. [online] Available at: https://www.safetydifferently.com/wp-content/uploads/2018/12/RestorativeJustCult ureChecklist-1.pdf [Accessed 21.03.21].
14. Al-Khalili J. (2017). *Quantum Mechanics.* Penguin.
15. Shorrock S, Leonhardt J, Licu T & Peters C. (2014). Systems thinking for safety: Ten principles. *A White Paper.* [online] Available at: https://www.skybrary.aero/bookshelf/books/2882.pdf [Accessed 13.03.21].
16. Woodward S. (2019). Moving towards a safety II approach. *Journal of Patient Safety and Risk Management,* 24(3): 96–99.
17. West M, Eckert R, Collins B & Chowla R. (2017). Caring to change. How compassionate leadership can stimulate innovation in healthcare. [online] Available at: https://www.kingsfund.org.uk/publications/caring-change [Accessed 10.04.21].
18. Stavros J, Cooperrider D & Godwin LN. (2016). Appreciative Inquiry: Organisation development and the strengths revolution. In *Practicing Organization Development: Leading Transformation and Change.* Wiley.

Chapter 8

Learning from Everything

Quantum Safety offers a radically different view of what is considered to be a Just Culture. Too often consideration about Just Culture is distilled down to a particular iteration of a checklist or algorithm. This narrow focus has allowed fundamental philosophical flaws to perpetuate unchallenged, such as the rationale that an organisation can have a Just Culture which creates an atmosphere of trust whilst only being applicable to the worst of events. Deep consideration of the philosophical underpinnings is crucial for progress. Change does not occur from theory alone. Quantum Safety addresses both the theoretical and experimental schools of thought. This chapter will explore how the Quantum Safety concept of Just Culture can be applied to help improve organisational learning and improvement whilst ensuring those involved are given the opportunity to heal and thrive. It shall also contrast how alternative views of Just Culture could be used in similar circumstances. To do so, scenarios will be used from within different industry sectors. These events are all based on real events researched for the purpose of this book, although all identifying aspects have been changed.

8.1 An Adverse Event in Healthcare

A lady arrives at her local emergency department. Upon investigation by a number of doctors the working diagnosis is that the lady is suffering from a brain haemorrhage. A trainee anaesthetist phones their consultant who is at home, to discuss transferring the patient to a nearby hospital that has the required surgical expertise to operate. The consultant anaesthetist asks what her GCS score is and is told by the trainee it is 10. The consultant says there

DOI: 10.4324/9781003175742-8

is no need for them to come into the hospital in order to intubate the lady and she can be transferred to the nearby hospital.

During the transfer the lady becomes more seriously unwell, her GCS score lowering to 6, and suffers consequences of being too deeply unconscious to protect her airway. Upon arriving at the second hospital the lady receives brilliant care, but sadly they are unable to save her life.

Following the immediate aftermath of the tragic event, the trainee anaesthetist was reprimanded by the consultant anaesthetist. The consultant was angered by the fact that the trainee had not told them that the patient's condition had been fluctuating and at times her GCS score had been as low as 8. The consultant also reprimanded the trainee for not emphasising the cause of the patient's low conscious level.

The GCS is the Glasgow Coma Scale. It is a well-validated, routinely used measure of conscious level, where 15 represents a normally conscious person, and 3 represents someone who has passed away. A level of 8 or below represents a patient who is unable to protect their airway. They are at risk of aspirating, where contents from the stomach move into the lungs and can cause pneumonia. Depending on the cause, GCS can fall at a consistent rate, can fluctuate up and down, or can fall and stay constant.

The real-world response was indicative of a blame culture. The trainee would undoubtedly have already felt responsible for the events. Being blamed for their decision within this event would do little to improve their ability to become as good an anaesthetist as possible.

8.1.1 Adopting a Just Culture

What would be the difference if this scenario was considered by applying the concepts of a Just Culture? There is no fixed concept of Just Culture, so it would be appropriate to explore how the concept as defined within Quantum Safety aligns with or differs from its predecessors.

8.1.2 Reason's Classical Just Culture

There are a variety of iterations of Just Culture algorithms or models based on James Reason's work.[1,2] This analysis shall follow the general principles that bind these models.

1. Firstly, there was no suggestion that the trainee intended to, or wanted to, harm the lady. Quite the opposite in fact.

2. The rules and procedures in place for this event are precise and clear. It could reasonably be argued that the trainee felt that they had followed the protocol by calling the consultant to check the correct course of action.
3. Next is the substitution test; would someone else likely have made the same or similar decision in similar circumstances? Another trainee, with the same training in a similar environment, could quite reasonably have acted in the same manner.
4. Also the trainee had no history of rule breaking.

The outcome would be a no-blame error. This response seems more appropriate than the real response meted out to the trainee, demonstrating the merit within the classical approach. The trainee is treated more fairly, which ought to help develop the atmosphere of trust Reason identified as being important.

8.1.3 Dekker's Restorative Just Culture

Exploring how Dekker's restorative approach would work in any such situation is difficult.[3] Conceptually, it is less transactional and more relational. The humanistic basis is an important development but does render any such comparison somewhat speculative. Accepting such limitations, we can consider how such an approach may have worked in this situation.

1. When considering who was hurt, the lady and her family clearly comes first. We have also identified the trainee would have been hurt by the event.

   Harm to the organisation's reputation and wider community harm may theoretically be possible but unlikely in this case.
2. What do the hurt people need? The grieving family may benefit from an apology, transparency and inclusion regarding the subsequent investigation.

   The trainee would also likely benefit from a compassionate response from her colleagues.
3. Whose obligation is it to meet the need? Dekker suggests the first victims, the family in this instance, are ideally willing to be involved in the restorative process. The trainee is willing to tell the truth and show remorse. The organisation should offer help and explore system fixes, although how the system is fixed is not outlined within this model.

4. Are people ready to forgive? Forgiveness is a process between people. It is not possible to speak to the emotional state of other people in such a situation. The grieving family could feel respected and soothed by the transparent and honest manner in which the hospital worked with them. It is possible that the candour serves only to anger the family in a manner in which they were not likely to have been had they not been told the details of the lady's treatment. This observation is not to advocate for non-disclosure of details or any other unethical behaviours, rather simply acknowledge that such disclosure could, in some circumstances, create harm rather than healing.

5. The final consideration is if the goals of restorative justice have been achieved. Moral engagement of affected parties, emotional healing, reintegration of the trainee and organisational learning are identified as such goals.

The efficacy of this approach is not clear given its subjective nature. Fleeting mentions of fixing systems and organisational learning are present, but how the system is understood or routes to learn are not signposted. The likelihood of an organisation with a historical blame culture possessing the required expertise and acumen to explore systemic fixes and garner organisational learning automatically is debatable. The logical extension to this is that for a Restorative Just Culture to be successful and achieve its goal, it must be predicated on a robust learning culture. This is the opposite view taken to James Reason and a less nuanced consideration of organisational safety culture than offered within Quantum Safety.

8.1.4 *Just Culture in Quantum Safety*

Both Reason and Dekker have significant merits to their approach to Just Culture, despite the clear divergences. We shall now consider how the Quantum Safety viewpoint would work in such a situation.

1. The trainee did act in a manner that they thought was correct. Given their actions were not beyond reasonable expectations and the outcome was clearly very sad, this would lead us to consider cultural factors.

2. It is also arguable that the decisions made by the trainee made sense at the time they were made in the context in which they were made. It is also reasonable to expect that another trainee with similar levels of

training would have done the same or similar thing. This would lead us to a conclusion that there was a potential for a pattern of behaviour that would indicate a situation where there is optimal systemic learning for the organisation. The focus of the learning is clearly signposted to understanding why those specific decisions made sense in that environment.

All three approaches, therefore, arrive at a conclusion that is not overly dissimilar. Whether the reader feels that the best outcome for the trainee was that their action is considered a no-blame error, that they should apologise, show remorse and be reintegrated or that their actions be considered an opportunity to learn is a personal decision.

Just Culture within Quantum Safety is not confined to these considerations. The consultant has, so far, not been included within this process, apart from their actual response which was to reprimand the trainee. Within the Quantum Safety approach we would consider the following:

1. For the same reasons as the trainee, the consultant would've felt like they were doing the right thing, but given the nature of the outcome we are led to consider the cultural factors surrounding their decisions.
2. Whilst it could be argued that their decision made sense at the time, it is less likely that another consultant would've made the same decision. This requires a little more detailed examination of the event.

   The consultant asked what the patient's GSM score was. They failed to ask whether this had been fluctuating. This piece of information was not ascertained and would have changed the medical picture and reaction. A trainee may not have understood the importance of this piece of information and so did not volunteer it, instead of answering directly the question asked.
3. The consequence of this is that we now reflect on the question of ownership. The outcome of which would be to reflect on the degree to which the consultant failed to fulfil their professional responsibility. This is not to say that the consultant was reckless or ought to be punished but recognise that their professional standard had fallen below what would be considered acceptable.

   The truth is that had the consultant considered more comprehensively the potential medical picture based on the information provided, the lady would've received more appropriate care and placed her at less risk.

If we applied Reason's classical approach, the outcome would've likely been a negligent error which is congruent to the Quantum Safety analysis. The restorative approach is less clear. The consultant did not consider themselves to be harmed, so even if others disagreed, the effect any process would've had on them is likely to be minimal. People who used to work within a blame culture are less likely to take responsibility for actions, including being hurt themselves. It is hard to reintegrate someone that does not accept *casus belli* or the need for personal restoration in the same manner that grieving families may never be willing to forgive irrespective of the best efforts of the organisation.

It is also important to recognise another substantive part of the process and the care the lady received has, until now, been ignored. The team at the second hospital provided outstanding care in a very difficult situation. The classical Just Culture approach literally has nothing to say about these people or their professionalism. The silence of Newtonian Safety prevails in the absence of failure.

Restorative Just Culture also is not particularly designed to consider these actions. At the most generous consideration, we could argue that this team would have been hurt by the loss of the patient and so psychological first aid may be required. This is a valid and important consideration to which we will return in Chapter 11.

Just Culture within Quantum Safety does not exclude this team. Their excellence is clearly recognised within this approach so that even in this tragic chain of events, the organisation is able to capture learning from what went well within this team. This demonstrates why the idea of a Just Culture and a Learning Culture should be considered as entangled, and the flaw of creating an approach that requires one to proceed in order for the other to prevail.

8.2 An Adverse Event in Rail

At the end of a long shift, at 1 am, a train driver berthed their train at Sidings within the rail depot. To get from Sidings to the main depot area (in order to exit the depot) staff must pass through a "restricted area" on foot. It's a narrow walkway within the depot which is close to the live tracks. It would be very difficult to avoid contact with a train if it passed through when walking through.

To keep the staff safe, they are required to call the depot controller on the radio to request permission to pass through the restricted area. The depot controller is responsible for controlling depot train movements and access to the depot for works. Before they grant permission, the depot controller needs to isolate the power to the conductor rail so that no trains are able to pass through in order to make it safe for staff to walk through.

The train driver called the depot controller to request permission but struggled to make contact. They also stated they only had one reception bar on their handset. At the fifth attempt they got through to the depot controller and requested permission to pass through the restricted area. The depot controller responded, telling the driver to "standby," meaning to wait. The train driver proceeded through the restricted area.

Immediately after crossing the restricted area, staff are required to call up the depot controller to inform they are clear; however, the train driver waited until they'd left the depot area completely before calling up. At this point the depot controller realised that a procedural irregularity had occurred.

Early inquiries found that the train driver thought they had heard the word "granted" and so were given permission to cross the restricted area and all safeguards had been undertaken. They also identified that there were some radio hardware issues in the control centre that had been reported the night before. The fall-back process, if there are radio issues, is to call up using the company-issued mobile phone. Another train driver who was a few minutes behind the train driver within the incident in question did use this fall-back process as their radio was also unreliable.

8.2.1 Reason's Classical Just Culture

As with the previous healthcare example, the consistent constructs used within a classical Just Culture approach will be applied to this scenario. There are, however, some immediate limiting factors when applying such an approach to this scenario. Primarily, the algorithms that Reason's approach generates are predicated upon an assumption that harm has occurred. Nobody was hurt within this adverse event (although an argument could be made that there was organisational harm) and there was no loss as this event would classically be considered to be more akin to a near miss. Nonetheless, the philosophical underpinning of the classical approach can be applied.

1. There was no suggestion that the individual bore any malice or desire to place anyone at risk.
2. The consideration of whether the person knowingly deviated from a known rule is finely balanced. A limited reflection would identify that the system in place was clear and that the person knowingly deviated from it. This would lead us to a conclusion that the person had recklessly violated and a strong disciplinary response would be appropriate.

   The principle of local rationality is not mutually exclusive from the classical Just Culture approach. A more progressive or mature analysis of events may reasonably allow us to conclude that the individual didn't knowingly break the rules at the time as they thought they were precisely following the rules.
3. If the analysis leads us to the second option, that there was no knowing deviation from the rule, we would then be required to consider the substitution test. It is reasonable to expect that anyone could've come to a similar conclusion in the same context if they thought they had heard that permission had been "granted." This would ultimately conclude the analysis, provided there was no prior history of poor actions or decisions, to a no-blame error.

8.2.2 Dekker's Restorative Just Culture

So how would a Restorative Just Culture approach consider this event?

1. Whilst nobody was physically harmed during this incident, there is a clear argument that organisational harm occurred. The train operator would not wish for their employees to place themselves in a potentially tragic situation and so would have been harmed by the events.

   Also, the harm does not necessarily have to be physical. The train driver may have been harmed if they felt they had worked in line with the procedures and still been placed in a position of unacceptable risk. The depot controller may also have experienced harm. They have the responsibility for controlling access and ultimately the safety of this process. The failure in this instance would likely have negatively impacted upon the depot controller.
2. What do those people need? Again, given the relational aspect of Restorative Just Culture it is impossible to say with any degree of certainty. The organisation would likely need to feel a greater degree of confidence that such an event would not reoccur. It is also quite

possible that an organisation may feel the need to have someone held responsible or punished. This is why a restorative approach requires a pre-existing learning culture to enable change with a leadership that is both compassionate and respectful. An organisation that formerly claims to adopt a restorative approach without this foundation can still blame unfairly.

Both the train driver and depot controller need to be truly listened to. They may also require some form of conciliation and support.

3. Whose obligation is it to meet these needs? The primary onus for this falls upon the organisation itself, especially their health and safety team. An effective investigation into the incident would provide the opportunity to identify how the system could be improved (see Chapter 9). This should be done in a manner that understands the process rather than be biased on the outcome and actively engage with the people involved in the decision-making (see Chapter 11).

It would not be surprising, however, that an organisation feels that it are able to meet all these needs by concluding an investigation that identifies individual training as the optimal mechanism to learn and improve.

4. As with the previous example in healthcare, whether people are ready to forgive is an entirely interpersonal proposition. It is impossible, therefore, to suggest whether this would be achieved via any of the options explored within this analysis.

This example identifies the similar potential of a restorative approach as the first example. It also reinforces the limitations.

8.2.3 *Just Culture in Quantum Safety*

The approach towards a Just Culture outlined within Quantum Safety is not affected by the lack of physical harm within this situation as it is focused on learning from all processes irrespective of outcome.

1. Accepting the principle that we ought to assume good intention until proven otherwise, the train driver acted in a manner in which they thought correct. The outcome, however, was not acceptable which would lead us to consider cultural aspects.
2. It was understandable as to how the decision made sense at the time. The train driver thought that they had been "granted" permission to

cross. The consideration of the substitution test is the same as the classical approach outlined previously. If someone thought that they had heard the word "granted" to their request, it is not unreasonable for them to think they have followed procedure and crossed.

This would lead us to recognise this was an opportunity for optimal systemic learning for the organisation and a potential pattern of behaviour. The initial inquiries identified some issues regarding the system of communication within this process, although the designed fall-back procedure of using a work-issued mobile phone worked with the train driver who followed shortly after. Closed-loop communication systems and agreed phraseology are recognised mechanisms in other safety-critical environments and may be worth consideration with this example.

This example shows the range of possibilities within the Just Culture concept. The classical approach may leave the train driver sanctioned due to their reckless violation or accepted as a no-blame error.[2] The restorative approach may enable the train driver and depot controller to feel respected and listened to, but requires a compassionate approach to safety leadership. The Quantum Safety approach is developed within a concept of learning rather than being dependent upon it pre-existing. This means it can help develop an approach that helps those harmed feel they have had the opportunity for redress and so develop an atmosphere of trust, but also identify tangible learning and improvement. This disconnect between the original intention of Just Culture and real-world application ceases to exist.

Questions for Reflection

What do you think are the most important factors within a Just Culture that you could use to improve organisational culture?

References

1. Reason J. (1997). *Managing the Risks of Organisational Accidents*. Ashgate.
2. Reason, J. (2004). *Aviation*. [online] Available at: https://www.skybrary.aero/bookshelf/books/233.pdf [Accessed 10.03.21].
3. Dekker S. (2018). Restorative just culture checklist. [online] Available at: https://www.safetydifferently.com/wp-content/uploads/2018/12/RestorativeJustCultureChecklist-1.pdf [Accessed 21.03.21].

Chapter 9

Beneath the Surface of the Lilypond: Understanding Causation in Complex Systems

It is time to return to the Lilypond. So far, our discussions have focused on safety at the macro level. It is imperative we have tools to understand accurately the nature of the modern, complex workplace. We also need to know what drives our performance and how those elements shape our organisational culture. For Quantum Safety to provide a platform to high-performance safety, it cannot solely operate at a conceptual level. Quantum Safety works at the micro level too. We need to understand the details within the science of work, not just characteristics. To do so, we shall plunge beneath the surface of the pond and try to understand what causes specific events or outcomes to manifest.

There are already a plethora of tools and models that try to offer insight into the nature of causation. Safety professionals have access to Accimaps, SIEPS, STAMP, FRAM and, of course, Swiss Cheese. Before we consider further what the best approach is to understanding causation, we need to go back to the first principles and consider the aim of such analysis in more detail. What is it that we are trying to find?

The most consistent answer to that question is to identify the root cause. This has resulted in root cause analysis (RCA) becoming a ubiquitous part of safety management systems, particularly when responding to adverse events.

The goal of RCA is "to find out what happened, why did it happen and what do you do to prevent it from happening again."[1] The Health & Safety Executive (HSE) defines the root cause to be "an initiating event or failing from which all other causes or failings spring. Root causes are generally management, planning or organisational failings."[1]

One widely advocated approach, included in official guidance from the HSE, is to adopt to achieve RCA through the 5 Whys, where "by repeatedly asking the question 'why?' (use five as a rule of thumb), you can peel away the layers of a problem to get to the root cause."[2] The Five Whys approach was initially developed by Sakichi Toyoda at Toyota and has since been widely adopted into systems of engineering, quality control as well as safety processes. The insights that this approach helped uncover were considered to be invaluable as Toyota improved their productivity, efficiency and safety within their production plants. The origination of the 5 Whys approach is instructive when considering its efficacy in complex systems as we shall soon see.

Many organisations have understandably established their investigative processes with this goal in mind. It is rare that anyone stops to consider whether this is the correct goal or an accurate frame to understand what has happened. It is rare but non-existent.

The concept of RCA has been subject to criticism within the academic circles. Peerally et al. identify eight challenges for RCA[3] These include the questionable quality of some investigations, political hijack and confusion about blame. The authors conclude that "RCA is a promising incident investigation technique borrowed from other high-risk industries, but has failed to live up to its potential in healthcare ... A key problem with RCA is its name, which implies a singular, linear cause."[3] Furthermore, Wiig et al. argue "investigation practice could therefore experiment more with variety in theoretical and methodological approaches to strengthen investigation quality."[4] In a momentary break from the critique of Safety II, Leveson, when considering the principle of causation, goes further stating that "there is no such thing as a root cause."[5]

This leaves an entirely unacceptable situation regarding a fundamental aspect of organisational safety, namely understanding why something happened. The national enforcing agency, the HSE, advocates a principle whose actual existence is doubted by highly respected academics and its methodology critiqued in safety-critical industries. Oblivious to this philosophical stand-off, RCA retains its hegemonic position. Which begs the question, should it?

9.1 Causation within the Lilypond

The increasing acceptance of arguments set out in Safety II has created friction with traditional approaches of causation analysis. Hollnagel cites this as "a 'hypothesis of different causes', namely that the causes or 'mechanisms' of adverse events are different from those of events that succeed."[6] This is a critical flaw of Newtonian Safety methodologies. In Newtonian Safety, only poor outcomes are investigated and analysed to identify future learning. But we now recognise that the system that creates adverse events also creates desirable outcomes. And in fact, for any system to survive, more of the outcomes must be successful than fail. Consequently, the approach to understanding causation must be applicable to *all* outcomes, not just a select few failings. Classical models such as the Swiss Cheese Model and the Domino Theory are only applicable to describing causation of adverse events and do not provide the opportunity to consider both Safety I and Safety II thinking.[6,7] RCA identifies what initiated a failure, but fails to acknowledge that it is the same management, planning and organisational factors that can achieve overwhelming success.

Quantum Safety does not accept that "there is no such thing as a root cause,"[5] because initiating or foundational activities can be identified for any event being analysed. Using the HSE's own guidance, what value is there in undertaking an investigation to identify the root cause if the root cause is nearly always the same? The learning from such an investigation is both flawed and limited in its current guise.

The Lilypond provides a conceptual framework that offers a new way of considering causation. Previously we considered the Lilypond Model as a whole and how that offered a more complete way of understanding organisational performance as well as the broad dynamics that created the organisational culture. Further consideration of the activities beneath the surface of the pond is required. The stem of each lily pad is a causational journey through time as the lily pad grows, irrespective of the outcome, and as such provides a more appropriate framework for developing an understanding of causation within complex systems.

The lily pad and stem represent the process of organisational output, the size and coloration of the pad symbolising the frequency and desirability of outcomes. Larger pads represent more numerous events. Brighter coloration represents increasingly more desirable outcomes. This view of the Lilypond, therefore, is not static as there is no stasis in organisational performance. Instead the plan view of the Lilypond continually waxes and wanes

Figure 9.1   Causation within the Lilypond Model.

with ever-changing coloration and size of lily pads. This more accurately allows for both the order and disorder of complex adaptive systems to be recognised.

The stem in its entirety should be considered representative of how that organisational output occurs (see Figure 9.1). Within this there will be many individual occurrences of this process being undertaken. We could consider it in the same manner as a stretch of motorway where a large number of drivers attempt the same journey, with ever-changing lane changes in reaction to traffic flow. It is this causational journey that we can analyse within the Lilypond Model, but to do so important work regarding systems thinking also needs to be considered and developed.

9.2 Understanding Different Types of Human Work

Hollnagel identifies the need to move away from Scientific Management Theory (SMT) and understand different types of work.[8,9] SMT was developed in the early twentieth century and demonstrated how a breakdown of tasks and activities into a linear process could be used to improve work efficiency. This became the basis for production lines and provided an understanding for how work was done. The synergy, therefore, with the understanding of causation by applying the Toyota-based 5 Whys is clear. The processes of RCA and the 5 Whys were designed to work for a linear production environment, which were complicated systems rather than complex. This is very different to the complexity of our systems in the modern workplace, and therefore these investigative approaches are not appropriately transferrable. Utilising these linear-based investigative processes places an emphasis on what would be ideal, or work-as-imagined, "thus provided the theoretical and practical foundation for the notion that work-as-imagined was a necessary and sufficient basis for work-as-done."[8]

Classical models of causation are predicated upon the principle of work-as-imagined. This linear approach is a concept of what should happen based on presumptions of the working environment and processes. Given the absence of complexity within the systems that they were trying to understand, this was not an apparent weakness. Work-as-imagined and work-as-done were easier to align. Behaviours and decisions made at the point of work, especially in complex systems, are often different from what was envisaged. Often the underlying presumptions that predicated the work-as-imagined turn out to be inaccurate or false. Work-as-done acknowledges that people innovate and amend practices frequently. These adaptive behaviours sit at the end of the Continuum of Human & Organisation Performance and were considered in more detail within the Human Performance Foxtrot in Chapter 6. These variations are integral to understanding causation.

This shift in analysing work activities is considerable and important. CIEHF states that "the Human Factors perspective focusses on understanding how work is actually performed."[10] It feels difficult to imagine an approach that wouldn't be focused on this, but such is our Newtonian heritage. When considering the completion of a single-work activity, work-as-done could be viewed as a linear process, which may or may not be the same as work-as-imagined. We are reminded of the bricklayer working in their simple system (see Chapter 2). When repeated, the process of this individual work activity becomes increasingly varied, and consequently work-as-done becomes less linear when not taken as an isolated, single-work activity.[11] Shorrock also identifies work-as-prescribed and work-as-disclosed[12] (see Figure 9.2). Work-as-prescribed is the formalisation of work-as-imagined. Work-as-disclosed is what we say and how we write about work. Whilst these observations about types of work are valid and useful, the best learning can be achieved by focusing on the work that actually happens, work-as-done, as well as understanding the work that it was thought would happen, work-as-imagined.

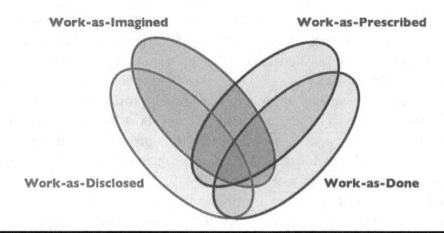

Figure 9.2   Different types of human work.

9.3 When Causation and Complexity Meet

When work-as-imagined and work-as-done are treated as discrete or estranged processes, they will remain so, even if at times they are perfectly aligned. Approaches, such as those proposed by CIEHF, have merit but lack the nuance required to truly understand causation in complex systems. This limits the opportunities to learn from outcomes as much as we ought to, as it is the relationship between these types of work that offers the greatest insight into understanding causation. Suggestions to focus solely on work-as-done are misguided, as work-as-done does not occur without work-as-imagined.[10] Work-as-imagined creates the frame for the work undertaken and establishes the expected outcome and process. Behaviours observed as work-as-done occur as a result of trying to make work-as-imagined a reality. These types of work do not just overlap at times. They are indelibly linked throughout and it is not possible to develop an understanding of "why did that decision or behaviour make sense at the time" without understanding how the relationship between these types of work created the environment in which the decisions were taken.[13]

In Complexity Science there is a concept called "teleologies." This is the term given to causal frameworks. "A teleological cause is an answer to the 'why' question. Why does a particular phenomenon become what it becomes?"[14] This is clearly a relevant notion to consider when analysing causation in complex systems. Applying an understanding of teleologies, and the potential relationships between different types of work, allows the complexity of events to be more accurately considered. This enables the development of a richer understanding of organisational outcomes which demonstrates that the current widely accepted approach that work-as-imagined is an unhelpful fantasy and the value lies in understanding work-as-done is, at best, incomplete.

Formative teleologies assume movement to a known future. These can be traced back to pre-Darwinian times where "there was a general sense of life changing to a plan."[14] The origin of cause and effect owes at least as much to a certain religious element as it does the development of industrial processes. When considering the nature of organisational performance, the lure of adopting mechanisms that are based on a formative teleology is understandable. Every organisation and every task will have a sense of purpose that should lead to a definable known state. Narrow applications of systems thinking subscribe to this idea of formative teleology. Safety III also appears to use this concept, stating, "When an accident occurs, the system (including the human operators) did not work the way I expected it to work."[5]

In complex systems the outcome is unknown. The outcome of the Cuban Missile Crisis, or a specific play by the All Blacks rugby team, is not pre-ordained (see Chapter 2). This would be considered to be a transformative teleology. Who better to explain transformative teleologies than Gwyneth Paltrow? Ms Paltrow is an incredibly versatile actor, so her ability to shine a light on the somewhat nebulous concept of teleologies and phenomenological emergence in complex systems should come as no surprise. In the 1998 film *Sliding Doors*, we see the journey of Ms Paltrow's character, Helen, through a period in her life. The film is predicated on the conceit of how Helen's life turns out depending upon whether she was able to catch a train on the London Underground. In one time line, she misses her train which means she returns home later and consequently doesn't find out about her partner's infidelity. The alternative time line follows Helen's life when she was less tardy and more aware. This film depicts the exact moment the emergence is activated as well as exploring the idea that the future is unknown when the interconnectivity of complex systems is properly considered. Understanding what actually happened, as opposed to what we expected to work, is crucial. This is why work-as-done offers valuable insights concerning organisational safety outcomes. It is not, however, the only source of valuable insights.

A consistent facet within complex systems is the importance of feedback. In this context, feedback does not mean a form of appraisal as it most consistently does, rather feedback is information within the system that can shape decisions made. This can come in the form of prior knowledge; how the work-was-done previously as well as whether it was considered to be successful or not. The knowledge of how a task should be performed, or the outcome that the organisation expects, can also act as feedback. Work-as-imagined, therefore, acts as feedback within the system.

Recognising this necessitates a shift from dismissing work-as-imagined as the fantastical view of work that offers little insight, based as it could well be on fantasy or ignorance. Irrespective of its veracity, work-as-imagined will still act as feedback. This is why it is the relationship between work-as-imagined and work-as-done that is integral to fully understanding causation and these cannot be treated as separate entities during any investigative processes. Rather than the distinction between known and unknown futures, our analysis benefits from understanding the work-as-done present within the context of aiming for an idealised future. Often the work-as-done adaptations or variations occur as someone is trying to help direct the present towards the idealised future of work-as-imagined. It is only possible to fully understand the past events by recognising the role that the idealised future had in shaping the environment or decisions that were made.

9.4 Adaptive Behaviours within the Lilypond

We now return to the Lilypond Model, and in particular its microscopic view of the lily pad stems. The stems of the lily pads consist not only of work-as-imagined, or just work-as-done, but both. Indeed, the additional labels of human work could also be considered (see Figure 9.3). The cross section of the stem, at any point in time of its development, would display all of the circles of human work, running alongside each other and overlapping and separating to varying degrees throughout the length of the lily pad stem.

Having identified the conceptual flaws of using linear methodologies to understand complex systems, we have established clear principles which any causational model should accommodate. These are counter to traditional approaches for understanding organisational safety outcomes.

1. Outcome classification – any model and process used must be equally applicable to all organisational outcomes, and not only suitable for examining adverse events.
2. Weighting of systems and processes – both work-as-imagined and work-as-done must be considered within the analytical process, as well as taking the effort to understand the relationship between them.

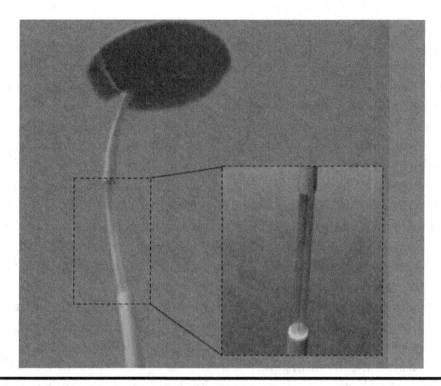

Figure 9.3 Work-as-imagined and work-as-done within the lily pad stems of the Lilypond Model.

The growth of the stem of the lily pad provides the concept of time as a process is undertaken, as well as being useful as an analogy for the different types of human work. We can then consider the varying alignment of these different types of work with each other, throughout the length of the stem of the lily pad. It is possible for a fully automated process, such as car manufacturer, to be repeated many times identically. It is not possible for humans to perform to such consistency, especially in complex systems. The same individual repeating complex tasks he is highly skilled at is unlikely to repeat the process exactly. The addition of multiple agents of a complex system will make this element of variation certain, as a result of crowd effects creating emergent phenomena.[15] One person's decision, action or execution will impact on another person's subsequent decisions, actions or executions as it is a source of feedback.[15]

The variation between work-as-done and work-as-imagined is a result of the interactions, including micro-interactions, identified within a complex system.[16] Many of these demonstrate a deviation from work-as-imagined but will not necessarily have an impact on the overall outcome. This would be considered non-causal variation. Consider a construction company that has to install pipework to connect gas to the houses they are building. As part of their safe system of work, the site manager is required to issue a permit to work to teams working in the excavation installing the gas pipe. The permit is issued to the ground workers, but some parts of the document are not signed or filled out comprehensively. The work, however, is carried out without issue. This is a clear deviation from work-as-imagined, within a safety-critical process, but not likely to be directly causal in the event of an adverse incident.

In this scenario, feedback will impact future behaviours. In the first instance, the site manager may decide in future similar situations, it may be acceptable to erode the safety-critical documentation, because an acceptable outcome was still achieved despite having deviated from work-as-imagined. This is what Diane Vaughan called "normalisation of deviance"[17] and why Dekker considered such actions as "seeds of failure."

There will be some variation from work-as-imagined that significantly changes the outcome. This is causal variation. In the example above, the failure to apply due diligence to the planning and information flow required within the work installing the gas main might mean that the opportunity to identify the dangers involved is missed. The groundwork team adopts a strategy to scan the work area for potential other utilities and pipes, which is insufficient. Unfortunately, a cable is subsequently damaged during the excavation. In this example, the variation from work-as-imagined by insufficiently scanning the ground before excavating impacts on the outcome.

Both these examples would apportion some liability applying Newtonian Safety methodology, such as RCA, to the individuals due to their deviation from known rules or procedures. This binary approach evidently doesn't work in complex systems as it fails to take into account the importance of understanding the role of adaptive behaviours within the Human Performance Foxtrot (see Chapter 6). The separation between the two parts of the stem is not necessarily an indication of poor professional behaviour. People often innovate or adapt from the prescribed system in order to effectively achieve the ideal outcome. A violation or deviation from work-as-imagined is not, therefore, inherently bad or undesirable, as we saw with the example of the Round the World yacht crew in the Human Performance Foxtrot. The learning and improvement within the system is more likely to be gained by conscious effort applied to understanding why the separation occurs, what the outcome of that deviation is and why the environment made the decision acceptable in the context within which it was made. This investigative process can be best achieved by developing a truly Just Culture which is predicated on learning rather than liability.

9.5 Developing Causal and Non-causal Variation

By embracing the two principles identified earlier, a more effective approach to understanding causation is possible. This can be done by recognising the importance of variation within the lily pad stems of the Lilypond Model.

There could be a stem within the Lilypond that represents the task of installing the infrastructure for a gas provider, including creating the excavation, installing the pipework and backfilling the excavation at the end of the task. The work-as-imagined part of the stem would be consistent and rigid, representing the established working protocol. The work-as-done part of the stem would unpredictably and continually diverge from and align with the work-as-imagined part of the stem, and this movement would differ each time the work is undertaken. The cross section of the stem would have, therefore, a circular work-as-imagined strand and a circular work-as-done strand, which continually overlap and separate throughout the length of the stem (see Figure 9.4). At times there will be more overlap or convergence between the types of work, at others the variation would be signified by a greater distance between them. The stem, therefore, consistently shifts in nature and shape throughout time and repetition. Consequently, any causal analysis process that tries to offer definite and fixed outcomes should be treated with caution. An approach that offers an analysis based on a probabilistic rather than deterministic nature would be more appropriate within complex systems. Rather than find a "singular, linear cause,"[1] we move to ask "of all the variations that have occurred, which were the ones that have most likely and most significantly contributed to this outcome?"

In Safety II, Hollnagel states that performance variability is inevitable but also useful, and so requires management. Typically, Leveson critiques this in Safety III adding that this is "quite difficult to do in system engineered design."[5] This is true. It also shows why understanding the implications of the Human Performance Foxtrot is important. Systems thinking, when reduced to pure engineering outputs, is insufficient when considering behaviours within a complex adaptive system. Quantum Safety recognises the importance of both social and technical interventions to manage risk within a socio-technical system. This is an approach that isn't as widely advocated as one may reasonably expect given the nomenclature. Quantum Safety also

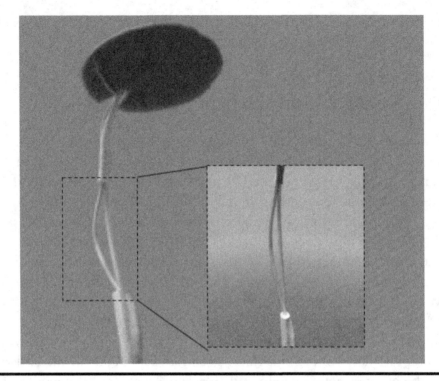

Figure 9.4   Work-as-imagined and work-as-done within the Lilypond Model.

agrees with Leveson's conclusion that the ultimate goal ought to be a system designed so that "performance variability is safe and conflicts between productivity, achieving system goals and safety are eliminated or minimized,"[5] provided the broad concept of systems thinking is adopted. This is not the case in many safety-critical environments currently and the approach outlined within Quantum Safety will be instructive in understanding where the systemic issues are.

Applying this concept of causal and non-causal variation remains subjective in nature, in the same way in which Swiss Cheese Model and other models of causation are. The difference from previous processes of causation analysis is that the focus on what is being analysed and in what context it has occurred, is a complete shift in safety thinking. It may be possible, however, to move from a purely conceptual framework. To this end the work of David Smith is of particular interest. Smith has adopted a sophisticated mathematical modelling analysis for complex adaptive systems with multiple agents.[18] His modelling has enabled to help predict behaviour within complex systems, creating corridors (Future-Casts) along which the system is likely to move. The width of these corridors is called characteristic stochasticity, and their average direction called characteristic direction. Characteristic stochasticity would provide insight into how much flexibility is required within the system and would be best understood whilst viewing the dance floor that Vincent and Amalberti[19] provided (see Chapter 6). Characteristic direction would offer a sense of projection between work-as-done and work-as-imagined, indicating how the lily pad was likely to appear or the kind of outcome we were heading towards.

Smith's approach is non-deterministic and instead indicates the probability of future order or disorder occurring within a complex system, "without knowing what individual objects are each doing – he can produce such corridors into the future … with remarkable accuracy.[15] Smith's work begins to bridge the conceptual framework with an empirical one, providing a potential methodology for identifying which variations are causal and most consequential for organisational learning.

This new view of causation analysis allows the true nature of behaviours within complex adaptive systems to be understood. It also helps safety professionals to move away from the doctrine of root cause analysis. Importantly, this extension of the Lilypond Model does not jeopardise its accessibility but does increase its applicability as well as consequential organisational safety learning.

So how do we do that?

Questions for Reflection

1. What are the current approaches to investigations within your organisation?
2. Do you think they provide an opportunity to identify areas that need to be improved within the organisational systems?
3. How is the nature of complexity within the workplace addressed within the investigation?

References

1. Health and Safety Executive. (2001). *Root Cause Analysis; Literature Review.* [online] Available at: https://www.hse.gov.uk/research/crr_pdf/2001/crr0132 5.pdf [Accessed 03.03.21].
2. ACT Academy for NHS Improvement. (2018). Quality, service improvement and redesign tools: Root cause analysis using five whys. [online] Available at: https://improvement.nhs.uk/documents/2156/root-cause-analysis-five-whys.pdf [Accessed 20.2.21].

3. Peerally MF, Carr S, Waring J & Dixon-Woods M. (2017). The problem with root cause analysis. *BMJ Quality and Safety*, 26: 417–422.
4. Wigg S, Braithwaite J and Clay-Williams R. (2020). It's time to step it up. Why safety investigations in healthcare should look more to safety science. *International Journal for Quality in Health Care*, 32(4): 281–284.
5. Leveson N. (2020). *Safety III: A Systems Approach to Safety and Resilience.* MIT Press.
6. Hollnagel E. (2016). Resilience engineering: A new understanding of safety. *Journal of the Ergonomics Society of Korea*, 35: 185–191.
7. Hollnagel E. (2014). *Safety-I and Safety-II. The Past and Future of Safety Management.* CRC Press.
8. Hollnagel E, Wears R & Braithwaite J. (2015). *From Safety I to Safety II: A White Paper. The Resilient Health Care Net: Published simultaneously by the University of Southern Denmark.* University of Florida and Macquarie University.
9. Taylor FW. (1911). *The Principles of Scientific Management.* Harper.
10. Chartered Institute of Ergonomics and Human Factors. (2020). Achieving sustainable change: Capturing lessons from COVID-19. [online] Available at: https://ergonomics.org.uk/Common/Uploaded%20files/Publications/Sustainable-Change/CIEHF-Achieving-Sustainable-Change.pdf [Accessed 03.02.21].
11. Seidling HM, Lampert A, Lohmann K, et al. (2013). Safeguarding the process of drug administration with an emphasis on electronic support tools. *British Journal of Clinical Pharmacology*, 76(Supplement 1): 25–36.
12. Shorrock S. (2016). The varieties of human work. [online] Available at: https://humanisticsystems.com/2016/12/05/the-varieties-of-human-work/ [Accessed 03.03.21].
13. Shorrock S, Leonhardt J, Licu T & Peters C. (2014). Systems thinking for safety: Ten principles. *A White Paper.* [online] Available at: https://www.skybrary.aero/bookshelf/books/2882.pdf [Accessed 13.03.21].
14. Stacey, R. (2000). *Complexity and Management: Fad or Radical Challenge to Systems Thinking?* Routledge.
15. Johnson N. (2007). *Simply Complexity: A Clear Guide to Complexity Theory.* Oneworld Publications.
16. Woodward S. (2019). Moving towards a safety II approach. *Journal of Patient Safety Risk Management*, 24: 96–99.
17. Vaughan D. (1996). *The Challenger Launch Decision: Risky Technology, Culture, and Deviance at NASA.* University of Chicago Press.
18. Smith DMD & Johnson NF. (2006). Predictability, risk and online management in a complex system of adaptive agents. [online] Available at: https://core.ac.uk/download/pdf/44113917.pdf [Accessed 01.03.21].
19. Vincent C & Amalberti R. (2016). *Safer Healthcare.* Springer.

Chapter 10

Learning When We
Don't Dock in the Bay

Quantum Safety considers safety as an integrated aspect of high performance. It would be logical, therefore, for this book to map to the Performance Continuum. The early chapters of the book have reviewed safety philosophically by considering the current New Views of safety as well as complexity science to identify the need and scope for Quantum Safety. This aligns with the Philosophical Realm and hopes the reader also helps with the translation from theory to practice. The Lilypond Model and the Performance Continuum begin to translate Quantum Safety into the Organisational Realm with special consideration for the role of a Just Culture. The final part of this book will consider more the applied nature of Quantum Safety, rather than theoretical. We will consider more the nature of interactions within complex systems and how the Personal Realm of the Performance Continuum can be influenced and shaped. To begin to do this, we shall explore how the idea of causal variation analysis can be utilised within the real working environment.

10.1 Causal Variation in Practice

Applying the principle of causal and non-causal variation analysis within the workplace should not require any greater degree of technical understanding than RCA. It is the understanding of behaviours within complex adaptive systems and the consequential shift in focus that will create substantial change in understanding of causation. An investigation applying the concept of causal variation analysis (CVA) would follow a five-step process to achieve a full understanding of the nature of the causation stem (see Figure 10.1).

10.1.1 The Plan

Hollnagel argues that understanding causation should focus on work-as-done rather than work-as-imagined due to the increased complexity of work environments, or "systems that are real rather than ideal."[1] This view reduces the potential learning. A more complete application of complexity science recognises the importance of work-as-imagined as a source of feedback within the system. It is imperative, therefore, that the idealised system is understood first. This strand of the stem is just as important.

10.1.2 The Event

Once the idealised system is understood and the nature of feedback it provides within a complex system is understood, attention can turn to work-as-done. In this sense feedback is the technical term that refers to information within the system, not a form of appraisal. Specifically, when considering investigations of adverse events, work-as-done could become as elusive as work-as-imagined. The distinction of work-as-disclosed is important. Rather than being a distinct strand as suggested in the varieties of human work[2] it may be more accurate to consider work-as-disclosed as a fuzzy outer layer of work-as-done. This can hide or reveal a central truth we seek to understand. It can allow work-as-done to be as based in reality as work-as-imagined. Sometimes, therefore, understanding work-as-done may require an approximation or subjective judgement.

In a truly Just Culture, the distinction between work-as-done and work-as-disclosed should become less discrete. In organisations where there is a high degree of trust and psychological safety[3] there should be little or no difference between work-as-done and work-as-disclosed.

When considering work-as-done it is important to understand when, and why, the work changed from work-as-imagined. It is also crucial that decisions are analysed in the context in which they were made, and we understand why they made sense at the time.[4] Within this the interactions between different agents of the complex system, or different creatures within the Lilypond, should be closely analysed.

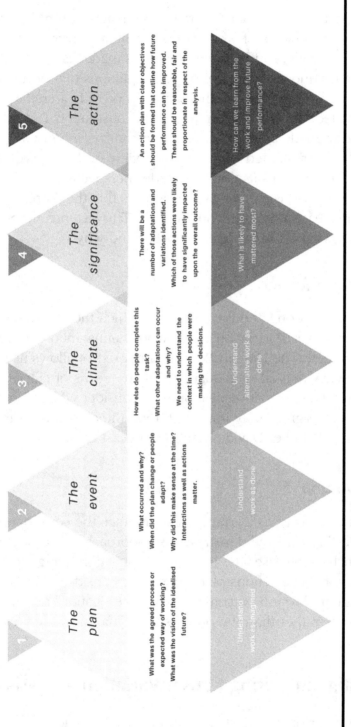

Figure 10.1 Causal variation analysis in practice.

10.1.3 The Climate

Work-as-imagined is not the only source of feedback within the complex system. Alternative versions of work-as-done will also form a considerable form of feedback. Understanding why decisions made sense at the time requires a broader understanding of other adaptations that occur when completing the same or similar tasks. This will help provide a credible answer to what Reason called the Substitution Test.[5] The Substitution Test asks if someone else would've made a similar choice in a similar circumstance. Often this consideration is restricted to a subjective view of the decision-making within the task under investigation. A broader perspective into the nature of the way in which work is carried out recognises that the work-as-done stem continually varies each time the work is done. This extends the Substitution Test to question what other adaptations occur and why.

10.1.4 The Significance

Both within work-as-done and the climate in which the task is generally undertaken, a number of variations from work-as-imagined will have potentially been identified. The Human Performance Foxtrot allows us to move from a narrow view that all such adaptations are "seeds of failure."[6] The challenge, therefore, in any investigation is to consider which variations are most likely to have significantly impacted upon the overall outcome. These are the moments that alter David Smith's Futurecast corridor.[7]

10.1.5 The Action

An approach that prioritises learning must embrace the consequential change an investigation should instigate. An approach called RCA[2] has been developed which emphasises the importance of action being created as part of an investigation.[8] The actions planned should consider fully the instinctive bias that hindsight plays on outcomes of the investigation[9] resultant of the focus on outcome rather than the process that Quantum Safety eschews.

10.2 Investigating Using Causal Variation Analysis (CVA)

There are a number of investigative techniques and models used within safety-critical industries. Some do not require a significant degree of expertise, such as Accimaps, whilst others, such as Hollnagel's Functional Resonance Analysis Method (FRAM), do. Adopting a CVA approach is not incompatible with such models. RCA, however, is the dominant methodology. It's ease of use helps maintain this hegemony. If safety-critical industries are going to improve their ability to learn from adverse events in complex environments, therefore, a CVA approach must be as simple to execute as RCA.

To outline how this may occur, we shall explore a real-world example and how the five steps to CVA explained here will work. As with all such examples, there will be a balance to strike between accuracy, fidelity and privacy. The information used consequently will all be from information within the public domain and reported in respected media outlets.

10.3 The Wakashio Grounding

On 25 July 2020, the Wakashio bulk carrier became grounded on a reef off the south of Mauritius. Subsequently, over 1,000 tonnes of fuel were spilled into a lagoon. This took place near two environmentally protected marine ecosystems as well as a wetland of international importance, the Blue Bay Marine Park reserve. The Mauritian government subsequently called the spill a national emergency.[10]

Before we undertake the CVA approach, it is worth reflecting upon the Human Performance Foxtrot (see Chapter 6). When exploring the idea of the Foxtrot, the example of adaptive behaviours within a Round the World yacht race was provided where people chose not to follow the protocols entirely in order to improve both safety and performance. The extent of adaptive behaviours was hypothesised to be significantly different from other aspects of the maritime industry such as bulk carriers and haulage where there would be less perceived need to adapt and an approach nearer the ultra-safe domain of the Vincent and Amalberti dance floor would be possible. The Wakashio grounding, therefore, should have been operating nearer the ultra-safe part of the dance floor. Classical systems thinking approaches would expect it reasonable to be able to create a series of processes and protocols that minimise the likelihood for adaptive behaviours. This event may be insightful when considering the accuracy and the validity of such classical thinking.

The Wakashio was owned by a Japanese transport company, Mitsui OSK Lines (MOL). The chief officer of the vessel was Mr Hitinamillage Tilakaratna

Subodha, who was second most senior rank. The most senior was the ship's captain, Mr Sunil Kumar Nandeshwa.

10.3.1 The Plan: Wakashio

The plan, or work-as-imagined, was relatively simple. The Wakashio was travelling across the Indian Ocean East to West heading to Brazil from Singapore. The passage plan was for it to travel past Mauritius at a range of 22 nautical miles. The standard speed for a bulk carrier ship at sea is 11 knots.[10]

10.3.2 The Event: Wakashio

On 25 July 2020, the Wakashio bulk carrier became grounded on a reef two nautical miles off the south of Mauritius.

The journey had not been uneventful upon departing Singapore on 14 July. According to data from British satellite analytics company, Geollect, the first issue the Wakashio experienced was on 15 July. The vessel deviated from the main shipping routes, moving from 14 nautical miles off the Indonesian coastline to around 4. On 17 July, the Wakashio ground to a halt and drifted from its supposed direction for five and a half hours. During this time, there were four transponder signals detected. This is incredibly unusual. AIS transponders should be detected every minute. There were no issues with satellite coverage in the region at that time. An expert at Geollect stated that a full engine failure alongside a full bridge electrical systems failure could account for both the lack of power and transponder signals.[11]

In 20 July, fuel samples taken in Singapore reached the laboratories at MOL. The analysis showed that some of the key parameters of the fuel exceeded ship's engine safety guidelines. The Wakashio reduced its speed by 15% and made a turn 13 degrees towards Mauritius.[11]

On 24th there was another course correction, albeit a minor one in comparison to the change on the 20th. During a subsequent press release from MOL, this correction was the reason provided to explain why the Wakashio was 5 nautical miles rather than 22 nautical miles from the coastline.[11]

On 25 July, the Mauritan fishing village of Mahebourg was 20 nautical miles from the Wakashio. The Wakashio was also heading directly towards it. Thankfully, the Wakashio slowed down and veered south.[11]

During the legal proceedings, more information came into the public domain. Both Subodha and his boss Nandeshwa gave evidence. MOL also supplied more information. All this would be considered to be work-as-disclosed rather than work-as-done – the fuzzy, speculative outer layer of our causal stem.

Subodha said that his captain, Nandeshwa, had asked him to move closer to the coast in order to get Wi-Fi coverage. This was something that Nandeshwa did routinely it was claimed.[12] Nandeshwa claimed the fault lay with his first officer, who had asked to go closer to the coast and had not followed his instructions when doing so.[12] Nandeshwa stated that going close to the shore to gain Wi-Fi access was good for crew morale as it enabled them to gain contact with their families.[13] MOL also have claimed that the crew were using a nautical chart to navigate which was not of sufficient scale to confirm accurate distances from the coast or depths. They also cited that there was a lack of watch-keeping by the crew.[14] This was corroborated by the evidence given by Mr Nandeshwa. The chief engineer, Preetam Singh, had been sitting in the pilot's chair on the bridge at the time of the grounding checking something on his phone. Finally, there was a birthday within the crew and a party had been held. Many of the crew were drunk at the time of the incident.[14]

10.3.3 The Climate: Wakashio

At the time of writing, most of the focus of the investigation and wider discussion has zeroed in on the decision to try to gain Wi-Fi access by moving closer to the shore. Nandeshwa has accepted that this was part of the decision-making at the time. He also acknowledged that he had done similar deviations many times over the years. In a similar occurrence, in 2019, his vessel came within five nautical miles of the Mauritian coastline and the local coast guard had communicated with his vessel to check the routing of the ship.[12] Indeed, there has been no explanation provided as to why the Wakashio deviated from its course on 15 July as it moved close to the Indonesian coastline. From this basis, Mr Nandeshwa may not be reflected in a particularly positive light.

There are also variations to consider with the broader navigation and the way in which the journey unfolded. The data available regarding global shipping lanes helps provide a very accurate picture of other examples of work-as-done.

10.3.4 The Significance: Wakashio

Cases of ships heading towards the coastline to gain access are "common" according to an industry magazine.[14] Additionally, the COVID-19 pandemic has resulted in many crews being kept at sea for much longer than their contracts stipulated and few ships have free Wi-Fi available for all. Andrew Craig-Bennett, a maritime journalist, noted: "Another thing that nobody talks about is the near-universal practice of ships taking every opportunity to pass within cellphone range of any coast that has a mobile phone system, i.e. anywhere. Wonder why people do that?"[15] With this awareness of the broader climate, rather than Mr Nandeshwa's decisions being a significant alternative from work-as-done, it could be argued that his decisions, whilst far from ideal, were entirely in keeping with the industry norm given the prevailing culture and systems.

By 20 July, the Wakashio was significantly further south than the main shipping lanes and experiencing difficulty. The data from satellites provides an uncanny similarity to the figure of causal variation in Chapter 9. The actions of 20 July present a significant variation from what could reasonably be expected. MOL has not publicly explained why the Wakashio drifted for so long and lost contact via the transponders. Had the subsequent course correction of 13 degrees not occurred on 21 July, the Wakashio would have not been within 350 nautical miles of Mauritius (see Figure 10.2).

From the information that is in the public domain, it is reasonable to try to ascertain why this variation occurred. The Wakashio had fuel which exceeded key safety parameters for the engine. The Wakshio appeared to suffer from both engine and electrical issues. Subsequently, the routing of

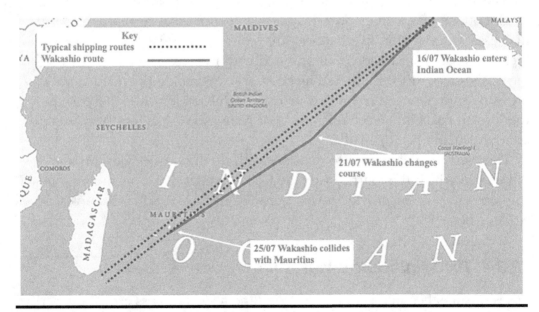

Figure 10.2   Wakashio route compared to the main shipping route.

the vessel significantly varied and communication from the Wakashio was limited.

10.3.5 The Action: Wakashio

At this point it is worth noting the outcome of preliminary investigations by MOL and the Panama Maritime Authority. The leadership on the vessel is identified as the primary causes of the incident due to a lack of "good seamanship practices" that would've allowed them to correct the situation.[14] They also noted the lack of supervision and distraction generated by the officer on watch.

Adopting a CVA approach does not absolve the crew or ignore their potential lack of professionalism. It does, however, take into account broader cultural norms which may have helped justify the decisions made in the context in which they were made. Such is the importance of feedback within a complex system. Indeed, rather than working towards an idealised future as discussed in Chapter 9, Mr Nandeshwa may have been working within what was considered to be a permitted reality, or what Rene Amalberti calls the "illegal normal."[16]

If Nandeshwa or Subodha were considered within a Just Culture (see Chapter 7), it is most likely we would identify their actions as a pattern of behaviour and an opportunity for optimal learning. The solution is not within the crew, but the system in which the crew were working. It should not be universal practice for vessels to navigate close to shore to access Wi-Fi. Crew members ought to have access to such provision consistently throughout their journey. The cost of such a change is dwarfed by the cost of the Wakashio grounding.

The significant variation in this instance was not the decisions made on 25 July, but five days earlier. More information is needed to ascertain what was happening on the Wakashio at this time. Also, the events surrounding the fuelling require greater clarity. The equipment being used to navigate and the decisions made regarding course corrections will also provide the information to begin to truly understand what most likely had a significant effect on this event happening. For the record, MOL stated in January 2021 that "there have been no reports whatsoever that the Wakashio had any mechanical or fuel problems in the period leading up to the grounding."[11]

The current, real-world situation is that Mr Nandeshwa and Mr Subodha have been placed under arrest and bail has been refused. If successfully prosecuted there will be potential fines of up to 30 million rupees (approximately $750,000) and five years' imprisonment.[17] It is hard to imagine a case persuasive enough to argue successfully that such a punishment will improve the safety of such operations in the future. It is a situation that is highly unlikely to be congruent with Quantum Safety principles, where learning from the process is more valued than judging people by the outcome.

Causal variation analysis does not exclude other models for analysing cause necessarily. CVA is designed to provide a more effective commonplace approach to the question of causation than the dominant RCA approach. This revision enables organisations to more effectively consider the nature of decisions in complex systems. This will allow opportunities to identify significant aspects of work-as-done and subsequently learn from adverse events more effectively. As suggested in Chapter 7, the propensity to blame frontline workers is as human as it is to err. This is why how we learn from events needs to be redefined.

References

1. Hollnagel E, Wears R & Braithwaite J. (2015). *From Safety I to Safety II: A White Paper. The Resilient Health Care Net: Published Simultaneously by the University of Southern Denmark.* University of Florida and Macquarie University.
2. Shorrock S. (2016). The varieties of human work. [online] Available at: https://humanisticsystems.com/2016/12/05/the-varieties-of-human-work/ [Accessed 03.03.21].
3. Edmondson AC. (2019). *The Fearless Organisation: Creating Psychological Safety on the Workplace for Learning, Innovation and Growth.* Wiley.
4. Shorrock S, Leonhardt J, Licu T & Peters C. (2014). Systems thinking for safety: Ten principles. *A White Paper.* [online] Available at: https://www.skybrary.aero/bookshelf/books/2882.pdf [Accessed 13.03.21].
5. Reason J. (2003). *Managing the Risks of Organizational Accidents.* Ashgate Publishing Group.
6. Dekker S. (2011). *Drift into Failure: From Hunting Broken Components to Understanding Complex Systems.* Ashgate.
7. Smith DMD & Johnson NF. (2006). *Predictability, Risk and Online Management in a Complex System of Adaptive Agents.* [online] Available at: https://core.ac.uk/download/pdf/44113917.pdf [Accessed 01.03.21].
8. National Patient Safety Foundation. (2015). RCA^2 improving root cause analyses to actions to prevent harm. [online] Available at: www.ashp.org/-/media/assets/policy-guidelines/docs/endorsed-documents/endorsed-documents-improving-root-cause-analyses-actions-prevent-harm.ashx [Accessed 19.11.20].

9. Henriksen K & Kaplan H. (2003). Hindsight bias, outcome knowledge and adaptive learning. *BMJ Quality & Safety*, 12(Supplement 2). ii46–ii50. http://dx.doi.org/10.1136/qhc.12.suppl_2.ii46-ii50

10. Degnarain N. (2020) How satellites tracked the fateful journey of the ship that led to Mauritius' worst oil spill disaster. *Forbes*. [online] Available at: https://www.forbes.com/sites/nishandegnarain/2020/08/09/how-satellites-traced-the-fateful-journey-of-the-ship-that-led-to--mauritius-worst-oil-spill-disaster/?sh=5ccb185a5b42 [Accessed 20.04.21].

11. Degnarain N. (2020). Satellites make new discovery about Mauritius oil spill ship Wakashio. *Forbes*. [online] Available at: https://www.forbes.com/sites/nishandegnarain/2021/01/22/satellites-make-new-discovery-about-mauritius-oil-spill-ship-wakashio/ [Accessed 20.04.21].

12. Insurance Maritime News. (2021). Differences emerge in court between Wakashio captain and chief officer. [online] Available at: https://insurance-marinenews.com/insurance-marine-news/differences-emerge-in-court-between-wakashio-captain-and-chief-officer/ [Accessed 20.04.21].

13. Safety 4 Sea. (2021). *Wakashio Captain Confirms Coming Close to Shore in Search of Internet*. [online] Available at: https://safety4sea.com/wakashio-captain-confirms-coming-close-to-shore-in-search-of-internet-connection/ [Accessed 19.04.21].

14. Chambers S. (2020). MOL comes clean on how this year's most high profile shipping accident occurred. *Splash247.com* [online] Available at: https://splash247.com/mol-comes-clean-on-how-this-years-most-high-profile-shipping-accident-occurred/ [Accessed 20.04.21].

15. Craig-Bennett A. (2020). The year of the petty bureaucrat. *Spalsh247.com*. [online] Available at: https://splash247.com/the-year-of-the-petty-bureaucrat/ [Accessed 20.04.21].

16. Vincent C & Amelberti R. (2016). *Safer Healthcare*. Springer.

17. gCaptain. (2021). Wakashio captain seeks bai in Mauritius's top court. [online] Available at: https://gcaptain.com/wakashio-captain-seeks-bail-in-mauritius-top-court/ [Accessed date 20.04.21].

Chapter 11

Continual Coaching: Moving from Outcome to Process

James Reason considered that a Just Culture would create a foundation for a learning culture (see Chapter 6). This was considered to be a valuable component of the broader sense of organisational safety culture. It is an important part of his work that is routinely overlooked. Quantum Safety moves away from the linear relationship between a Just and a Learning Culture, instead considers them to be entangled. Consequently, greater consideration needs to be given to the idea of what a learning culture is and how this can most effectively be achieved. Learning, in a formal sense, is an element within the Human & Organisational Performance Continuum. It is not reasonable to expect people to be able to maximise their potential without a mature approach to learning and development. We recognise that the best formal environments for learning enable individuals to be stretched and studies are based on work-as-done rather than work-as-imagined. This will enable the organisation as a whole to embrace and value such opportunities.

Within any organisation there are many more informal learning opportunities that can be a source of improvement for the individuals or the company. For most people it is these opportunities that shape the perception of organisational culture and their working environment to a far greater extent than any top-down approaches or mechanisms for learning or change. These informal learning opportunities require more analysis to ensure that they are congruent with the ideas of a Just Culture. Failure to do so can inhibit cultural change as organisational aims and values become incongruous to the work experience of most within the organisation.

DOI: 10.4324/9781003175742-11

Throughout the past 20 years the understanding of what constitutes effective feedback has evolved within education. Our understanding of systems thinking and Complexity Science has become greater. The New View Refraction (see Chapter 1) demonstrates the changes occurring within safety understanding, Quantum Safety significantly developing this further. In contrast to these changes, the communication modes used to embed these principles remain fixed. Investigative mindsets have not significantly changed since the development of Scientific Management Theory during the early twentieth century. Our approach to feedback formulation is still firmly wedded to the same principles developed 40 years ago.[1] To put it mildly, the walk and the talk have long ceased to be the same thing.

Given the inertia outlined previously regarding the development of a truly Just Culture (see Chapter 7), the effectiveness of the existing informal learning approaches needs to be re-evaluated. There is a clear need to overcome this communication barrier to cultural change. This does not mean a new model for feedback is required. Instead, a wider framework is proposed that can create a common language for learning, reflecting up-to-date thinking in educational as well as organisational performance and help normalise healthy improvement in the workplace.

11.1 How Learning Opportunities Are Utilised Currently

Quantum Safety recognises that proposing such a framework will be met with resistance within the workplace. Truly embracing learning throughout an organisation has been both glacial and sporadic. The existing methodologies used when there is potential to learn are firmly entrenched. To challenge this hegemony, potential learning opportunities will be examined and contrasted to evidenced best practice that ought to be applied to maximise learning.

11.1.1 Responding to Adverse Events

Most classical safety management systems value adverse events as important learning opportunities. This is perpetuated by the belief in Heinrich's Safety Triangle.[2] Near-miss reporting systems are designed with the expectation of obtaining information about events and situations affecting safety. Whilst this is not incorrect, both Safety II and Quantum Safety would consider this to be a limited perspective. The Lilypond Model creates space to enable organisations to learn from all events, irrespective of the colour of the emerging lily pad (see Chapter 3). To create a true learning culture, existing mechanisms designed to provide insights should be reconsidered so that the broader Quantum Safety view can be incorporated.

Furthermore, systems thinking should be adopted which appreciates the nature of adaptive behaviours within a complex adaptive system, as explored within the Human Performance Foxtrot (see Chapter 6). Most existing learning opportunities have become deterministic in nature. Individuals expect discrete packets of information will improve performance if acted upon. Such methods fail to appropriately address behaviours and processes within complex adaptive systems. In order to create real learning, and maximise the opportunity for improvement, the nature of complexity within the workplace needs to be taken into account.

In complex systems, individual actions or decisions cannot be learnt from in isolation. In Chapter 2 we explored how the micro-interactions within a complex adaptive system are similar to playing a game of Rock, Paper, Scissors; it is impossible to analyse whether someone's decision to select paper is optimal, without taking into context the other person's decision. This is understood as non-equilibrium dynamics.[3] Within such dynamics small variations from the equilibrium can produce significant differences in the state of the system.[3] Understanding these variations is key to learning and improving performance. The principle of causal and non-causal variation (see Chapter 9) outlines that such analysis is based upon understanding the relationship between both work-as-imagined and work-as-done.[4] The language of investigations has to be developed to recognise this shift in the understanding of causation.

11.1.2 Specific Feedback

A more individualised learning opportunity comes in the form of specific feedback. Feedback is an essential part of the development of individuals. There is a wide range of literature focusing solely on feedback across a range of industry sectors as well as in simulation training and workplace setting.[5,6] Cantillon and Jones, for example, state that "the primary purpose of continuing medical education is to maintain and improve clinical performance."[7] This stated purpose is unarguable. The scope of reference regarding performance improvement is open to greater debate.

There are a great number of models for feedback proposed within literature, most of which are derivations from the Feedback Sandwich and Pendleton's Rules.[1,8] The Feedback Sandwich wraps negative (or constructive) feedback with positive observations either side. Pendleton's Rules follow a similar dynamic but enable more collaboration. Firstly, the teacher asks what their student felt went well. This is followed by an acknowledgement of what the teacher also felt was positive. The student is then asked what they felt should be improved or done differently. Again, this is echoed, acknowledged and an alternative opinion potentially suggested by the teacher. Pendleton's Rules do importantly bring in the principle of collaboration for learning.[1] This is an important characteristic within Shein's Humble Leadership approach, advocating an environment of "ask, don't tell."[9]

The Feedback Sandwich and Pendleton's Rules, as well as their many derivations, are outcome driven. Applying the Lilypond Model, language is currently predicated on the event outcome or coloration of the lily pad rather than understanding the process that created it. If feedback is to enhance an individual's self-efficacy for making progress, the outcome should not prejudice the learning. The model proposed by Molloy has much merit to enable such a change. This model states that "effective feedback answers three questions; where am I going? (Feed Up) How am I going? (Feed Back) Where next? (Feed Forward)."[10] The "how am I going?" question should avoid the temptation to offer a review or score based on outcome but adhere to the principle of understanding the process.

Consideration also needs to be given on what the feedback should focus upon. If feedback focuses primarily on technical skills, an opportunity to learn and improve is potentially missed. Non-technical skills are equally as vital for performance. A deficiency in one field is accompanied by a deficiency in the other.[11] The micro-interactions within teams dependent on non-technical skills can, therefore, have a significant impact on performance as we saw with the example between the trainee anaesthetist and consultant in Chapter 8. Consequently, a framework should be developed to create an approach inclusive of both domains. Lefroy et al. offer a definition of helpful feedback as "a supportive conversation that clarifies the trainee's awareness of their developing competencies, enhances their self-efficacy for making progress, challenges them to set objectives for improvement, and facilitates their development of strategies to enable that improvement to occur."[12] This broad scope of understanding what feedback should be in the workplace is more beneficial for learning as it incorporates all of the predominant principles advocated by Schein, Molloy and Quantum Safety.[9,10]

11.1.3 Post Event Briefing

Briefings, sometimes referred to as safety huddles in some sectors, are a consistent form of team communication and can take on various structures or appearances. Briefings are short gatherings of any duration, event or time that can enhance awareness of potential problems.[13] At the start of a shift, briefings enable teams to clarify roles and establish a plan. This, therefore, focuses on work-as-imagined and work-as-prescribed. Following a shift, a debrief is an opportunity to analyse work-as-done.

Debriefs are typically classified as hot or cold; determined by their timing in relation to an event. A hot debrief occurs in close proximity to an event, typically as soon as most of the team members from the event are physically available to meet to debrief. Cold debriefing occurs in the days or weeks following an event. Hot debriefing can benefit from people's recollections being fresh, whereas cold debriefing can allow individuals time to reflect and collect additional information to enable a more detailed review of what occurred. Practitioners ought to be recognisant that the proximity to an event will also reflect the emotional state of the team and potential vulnerability. The opportunity to analyse and learn should not supersede the importance of safeguarding the members of the team.[14]

The structure of the debrief can adopt many models. Consequently, the effectiveness of these interventions is highly variable. Debriefing is the optimal event to amalgamate aspects of understanding complex adaptive systems as well as best practice in learning and feedback identified above, but most models fail to incorporate both aspects. An accessible methodology could significantly improve the fidelity of these interventions, providing real learning and cultural evolution within frontline service delivery teams.

11.2 Facilitated Learning and Improvement Conversations

We have seen that there are many existing vehicles for potential learning within organisations. We have also examined how some of these opportunities are conceptually flawed, reducing the potential to learn. A new approach to undertaking these processes is required to increase opportunities to learn within the dynamics of a complex adaptive system: Facilitated Learning and Improvement Conversations (FLIC).

The proposed approach to FLIC is to adopt a structured framework, not a prescriptive model. This will allow the principles within the approach to be applied across a greater number of situations, amplify learning potential and equip practitioners with a common language in line with modern thinking within teaching and learning. It is an approach that can be used as a framework for a debrief, language within an investigation into an adverse event as well as how to model feedback for individual development. This common language and approach shall act as a tangible manifestation of transformative leadership principles. It represents a shift from "a culture of do and tell" to one of humility.[9] This humble, compassionate leadership approach leads not to a question-and-answer session where the leader waits to see if the group share their predetermined judgement but a genuine, curious dialogue where the leader "listens with fascination."[15] This approach reinforces the mutualism identified as crucial to the creation of a healthy ecosystem within an organisational Lilypond.

Just Culture within Quantum Safety utilised the potential of Appreciative Inquiry. Appreciative Inquiry has been defined as "a philosophy, an approach, a process and a way of being for engaging all levels of an organisation."[16] One of its core principles is constructivism, where reality is constructed through language and it adopts a positive psychological approach. This shifts questions from a problem-solving focus to an appreciative focus: "how are you going to fix this?" becomes "what does it look like when you …?" FLIC should adopt similar appreciative language.

The first consideration before starting a learning intervention is whether the timing is appropriate to focus on analysis and review of events. Safeguarding all people takes primacy over learning. If there are members of the team who are considered to be at a potential risk of emotional harm from analysis immediately post adverse event, the intervention should be focused upon Psychological First Aid.[14] This recognition helps to ensure that the organisational culture helps people to have the opportunity to heal (see Chapter 7).

Having identified the opportunity and appropriateness for learning, FLIC can occur. The social construct of investigations and briefings places a bias towards a centralised power base for the person leading the intervention. This creates a hierarchy and an expectation of a top-down communication flow. The interventions will be more successful adopting a collaborative, flattened hierarchy allowing all members of the team to input and offer opinions, leaving the "do and tell"[9] culture and moving towards a more compassionate and inclusive approach. It is worth noting that high-performing teams in elite sports have successfully embraced this cultural shift; Sir Clive Woodward's World Cup-winning England team, the New Zealand All

Blacks and the San Francisco 49ers under Bill Walsh all adopted a principle that Woodward calls "teamship," an environment of ask rather than tell.[17-19]

This will be difficult to achieve if the team lacks psychological safety. Team members will be reluctant to raise difficult truths, especially if the issues lie higher within any perceived hierarchy.[20] Amy Edmondson identifies the "power of the apology."[20] By apologising, the leader can demonstrate humility and vulnerability, by acknowledging their fallibility they inspire others to do likewise and so enable people to speak up.

Having established the appropriateness for learning and establishing a trusting, safe space to enable a learning conversation, the consideration shifts to what the conversation should focus upon. Often these learning opportunities are centred on two concepts which are aligned with the Feedback Sandwich and Pendleton's Rules: what went well and what could have been improved. FLIC is a significant shift away from this mindset and adopts the principles of Molloy's model. FLIC requires flexibility in order to ensure it remains effective whilst also having a greater degree of applicability; it should not be considered to be akin to a communication matrix or checklist. Dependent on the context some aspects will be more valuable than others allowing interventions to be more greatly differentiated.

All such conversations should consider and focus on three aspects: adaptations, interactions and decisions.

11.2.1 Adaptations

Often, investigative processes start with the information within work-as-imagined and consequently work-as-prescribed. The notion of what went wrong is related to the idea of why there was deviance from the plan and why was it accepted. Why was work-as-done not exactly the same as work-as-imagined? This is classical Newtonian Safety in action. There needs to be a shift to embrace the principle of causal variation (see Chapter 9) and a full consideration of the Human Performance Foxtrot (see Chapter 6).

It is also worth noting that in a team acting without psychological safety there will be many low-trust behaviours. Within these teams, the work-as-disclosed during any investigative process will differ from the true work-as-done, as individuals will be reluctant to accept responsibility for fear of the consequences and disclose a version of events that places them at less perceived risk. The consequential learning will be impaired as a result. A common language and approach that helps embed behaviours that encourage psychological safety will improve long-term organisational learning and improvement.

Understanding adaptive behaviour in complex systems is a key component to understanding performance. The choreography and execution of the Human Performance Foxtrot should be a foundation stone to learning. Discussing the adaptations will provide an opportunity to recognise which adaptations mattered most. This helps to reveal potential systemic weaknesses and enable people to conceptualise and accept the nature of working in complex adaptive systems (Table 11.1).

11.2.2 Interactions

Adaptive behaviours are inconsistent depending on the individuals within the team. Furthermore, adaptations will be inconsistent within the same individual as they are likely to make different decisions in similar circumstances. There is learning to be gained from considering the work from a systemic perspective of adaptations. There is also learning to be gained from an interpersonal perspective of how cohesively the team operated. The performance of any team will be shaped by countless micro-interactions and it is important we understand what happened and how people felt working within the socio-behavioural aspect of their work. As Miller and Page

Table 11.1 Facilitated Learning and Improvement Conversations: Adaptations

Aim: Understand the relationship between work-as-done and work-as-imagined	
Concept to explore	Questions to consider
Understanding work-as-imagined and work-as- prescribed	Is there an accepted standard for the work undertaken?
	What information was briefed to the team before the work?
	Was there an agreed protocol or approach for the work undertaken?
Understanding work-as-done: Accepting variation	How closely did our work resemble the original plan?
	When did we change from this plan?
	Why did we feel this needed to happen?
Causal variation	Which of these changes do we feel had a significant impact on our work?'

explain on Complexity Science, "one and one may well equal two. But to really understand the nature of two we must know both about the nature of one and the meaning of and."[21]

To understand the micro-interactions is to try to know the nature and meaning of "and." The optimal team dynamic would allow people to feel comfortable to reflect and admit to behaviours that have not been interpreted or received as respectful or helpful. Within the sub-optimal reality, it will be difficult for many people to achieve this level of psychological safety. Initially, therefore, some of the questions posed within FLIC may be received better as opportunities for self-reflection than group discussion. It is important, however, that there is opportunity to recognise the importance of non-technical skills within team performance and scope to begin to challenge behaviours that are unhelpful or unacceptable (Table 11.2).

11.2.3 Decisions

It would be a reasonable assumption that for a majority of outcomes there would be effective learning and improvement encapsulated from the conversations based on understanding adaptations and interactions. There will, however, be some events where there is valuable learning to be acquired from the analysis of specific decisions made during the execution of the work. These may have been decisions that were highly unusual and helped

Table 11.2　Facilitated Learning and Improvement Conversations: Interactions

Aim: Understand the socio-behavioural effectiveness of the team performance	
Concept to explore	Questions to consider
Respectful affirmation	What did we do to help our team within this work?
	What did another member of the team do to improve the work?
	What should we repeat more?
Affirming respect	What is it like being on the receiving end of me?
	At any point was communication lacking some clarity?
	How appropriate was our language within our team?
	Was my behaviour, verbal and non-verbal consistently civil, professional and respectful?
	Is there anything we could consider changing?

to generate an excellent outcome that was otherwise unlikely or unexpected. There will also be times when specific decisions need to be understood in the context that they were made if they were felt likely to have negatively impacted the outcome.

Naturalistic decision-making (NDM) is a branch of human performance psychology that aims to describe "how people make decisions in real work settings."[22] It shifts away from traditional methodologies of optimal judgements based on probabilities and expected utility and seeks to offer insight into decisions made where goals may not be clear or the risk uncertain. There are eight factors that characterise decisions made in naturalistic settings: "ill-structured problems, uncertain dynamic environments, shifting, ill-defined or competing goals, feedback loops, time stress, high stakes, multiple players and organizational goals and norms."[23]

In many safety-critical environments, the complexity of the system presents many of these characteristics. For example, in healthcare, decisions are often made when the nature of the problem being presented by the patient is unclear; the human body is fundamentally a dynamic and uncertain entity, and there is no one clear optimal goal or outcome and there are multiple external and internal feedback systems. Also, the nature of the decisions is likely to be high stakes, and the decisions are made within the context of a team environment with multiple players. Consequently, many decisions made within complex systems share most of the characteristics making NDM an appropriate mechanism to understand work-as-done.

Our concept of whether a decision is good or bad is usually linked to the notion of taking the best option dependent on the probability of a good result. NDM lacks this analytical criterion. NDM is focused on understanding the process rather than the classification of outcome; "instead of tracing bad outcomes to human error as the end of the inquiry, NDM researchers have learned to treat human errors as the beginning of the investigation."[22] Whilst FLIC utilises NDM methodology as a basis for understanding events after they have occurred, NDM may also offer great value regarding improving organisational performance when applied to the training and development of non-technical skills and decision-making (Table 11.3).

An approach that considers safety performance to be an integrated aspect of high performance is the most significant shift in risk management for 50 years. It is not necessary, or even desirable, to expect such a seismic change to occur as a result of wide-scale training and education. Members of the organisation do not need to have an awareness of the New View Refraction or the fact that Complexity Science is not a synonym for difficult.

Table 11.3   Facilitated Learning and Improvement Conversations: Decisions

Aim: Understand why the decision made sense at the time	
Concept to explore	*Questions to consider*
Initial situation	How familiar was the situation the person found themselves in? How experienced was the person with this type of situation
	Would it have made sense at the time to get more information?
	How much time was available to make the decision?
Mental mapping	What was the expected sequence of events?'
	How uncertain was the situation?
	What alternatives were considered at the time⁷ Why were they not acted upon?'
	Was any feedback offered by any members of the team?
	What can we learn, organisationally or individually, from this decision⁷

Adopting a framework which can be utilised in a variety of settings, where there is potential to learn and one that is developed using such insights, negates such a requirement. FLIC is designed to provide such a solution and equip team members with a common language and framework. It shifts the focus from the outcome to the process. A learning culture requires continual coaching. FLIC is the language to create that.

Questions for Reflection

Within existing opportunities to learn and improve safety performance, how much of the approach or language adopted is rooted in a classical, Newtonian approach?

References

1. Pendleton D, Schofield T, Havelock P & Tate P. (1984). *The Consultation: An Approach to Learning and Teaching*. Oxford University Press.
2. Heinrich HW. (1931). *Industrial Accident Prevention: A Scientific Approach*. McGraw-Hill.

3. Sinervo B & Lively CM. (1996). The rock-paper-scissors game and the evolution of alternative male strategies. *Nature*, 380: 240–243.
4. Shorrock S. (2016). The varieties of human work. [online] Available at: https://humanisticsystems.com/2016/12/05/the-varieties-of-human-work/ [Accessed 03.03.21].
5. Swayer TL & Deering S. (2013). Adaptation of the US Army's after action review for simulation in healthcare. *Sim Healthcare*, 8: 388–397.
6. Archer J. (2010). State of science in health professional education: effective feedback. *Medical Education*, 22: 101–108.
7. Cantillon P & Jones R. (1999). Does continuing medical education in general practice make a difference. *BMJ*, 318: 1276.
8. Von Bergen CW, Bressler MS & Campbell K. (2014). The sandwich feedback method: Not very testy. *Journal of Behavioural Studies in Business*, 7: 1–13.
9. Schein E. (2013). *Humble Inquiry: The Gentle Art of Asking Instead of Telling*. Berrett-Koehler.
10. Molloy E & Bould D. (2013). Feedback models for learning, teaching and performance. In Spector JM, Merrill D, Ellen, J & Bishop, M.J (Eds.., *Handbook of Research on Educational*. Springer.
11. Riem N, Boet S, Bould MD, Tavares W & Naik VN. (2012). Do technical skills correlate with non technical skills in crisis resource management: a simulation study. *British Journal of Anaesthesia*, 109(5): 723–8.
12. Lefroy J, Watling C, Teunissen PW & Brand P. (2015). Guidelines: The do's, don't and don't knows of feedback in clinical education. *Perspectives on Medical Education*, 4: 284–299.
13. Deng M, Weiju C, Tianying P & Chunmei L. (2019). Effect of daily safety huddles on the reporting of adverse events and near misses. *American Journal of Nursing Science*, 8(3): 92–96.
14. Marmon LM & Heiss K. (2015). Improving surgeon wellness: The second victim syndrome and quality of care. *Seminars in Pediatric Surgery*, 24: 315–318.
15. West M, Eckert R, Collins B & Chowla R. (2017). Caring to change. *How compassionate leadership can stimulate innovation in healthcare [Internet]*. [Cited 21.03.21]. Available at: https://www.kingsfund.org.uk/publications/caring-change
16. Stavros J, Cooperrider D & Godwin LN. (2016). Appreciative Inquiry: Organisation development and the strengths revolution. In William Rothwell, Jacqueline Stavros, Roland Sullivan (eds.), *Practicing Organization Development: Leading Transformation and Change*. Chapter: 6. Wiley. pp. 96–116. DOI: 10.1002/9781119176626.ch6
17. Woodward C. (2004). *Winning!* Hodder & Stoughton.
18. Kerr J. (2013). *Legacy: What the All Blacks Can Teach Us About the Business of Life*. Little Brown Group.
19. Walsh B, Jamison S & Walsh C. (2009). *The Score Takes Care of Itself: My Philosophy of Leadership*. Penguin.
20. Edmondson AC. (2019). *The Fearless Organisation: Creating Psychological Safety on the Workplace for Learning, Innovation and Growth*. Wiley.

21. Miller JH & Page SE. (2007). *Complex Adaptive Systems: An Introduction to Computational Models of Social Life.* Princeton University Press.
22. Lipshitz R, Klein G, Orasanu J & Salas E. (2001). Taking stock of Naturalistic Decision Making. *Journal of Behavioral Decision Making*, 14: 331–352.
23. Klein G, Orasanu J, Calderwood R & Zsambok C. (1993). *Decision Making in Action: Models and Methods.* Ablex Publishing Corporation.

Chapter 12

The Way Ahead: Developing a Roadmap with Quantum Safety

Too often pieces of work that offer new theoretical or conceptual view point fail to adequately address the translational aspect. How do organisations adopt Safety II in practice? Just how different is Safety Differently? This is why Quantum Safety has consistently addressed both the theoretical and experimental school. In order to affect change it is not enough to offer a revision to the concept of Just Culture. Here we offer ideas as to how this would work in practice. It is this consideration to which we return in the final chapter. How will the world of Quantum Safety manifest in safety-critical industries?

Before this is possible, it is necessary to revisit the insightful work of Miller and Page.[1] Their elegant work on agent-based modelling compares the use of such models to maps (see Chapter 4). The need for veracity and insight requires balancing with accessibility, particularly regarding the complexity central to the analysis. The same fine judgement is required when considering the way ahead. It would be injudicious to attempt to offer an accurate portrayal of how Quantum Safety is applied in all safety-critical industries. As we know from Mary Uhl-Bien's work, complexity problems require complexity solutions.[2,3] This final chapter will provide a map, with a series of overlays, to be used in conjunction with the preceding tools and concepts to help people to explore Quantum Safety further.

DOI: 10.4324/9781003175742-12

12.1 Institutions and Doctrines

Progress is rarely linear nor immediate. By reframing the idea of organisational safety so significantly, it is clear there will be resistance. It is a process that has been repeated many times within scientific fields. Nicholas Copernicus published his book *On the Revolutions of the Heavenly Bodies* in 1543.[4] Within this Copernicus argued that the earth was not at the centre of the universe, but rather it rotated around the sun. This upset the Catholic Church as it directly challenged their scripture and teaching. The anger was sufficient that the church placed his book on a list of prohibited publications. The personal consequences for Copernicus were mitigated somewhat by the fact that he died shortly after publication. This author hopes that neither of these fates awaits this project.

1905 was witness to Albert Einstein's annus mirabilis. He published five papers, each of significant scientific value and progress. He did so whilst working at a patent office in Bern, Switzerland. The academic and political might of highly regarded institutions such as the Prussian Academy of Sciences were reluctant to recognise the advances made. In time it was Einstein himself who argued against the progressive thoughts of his contemporaries. Famously, he critiqued Heisenberg's Uncertainty Principle. Writing to Max Born in 1926, he stated, "the theory yields a lot, but it hardly brings us closer to the secret of the old one. In any case I am convinced that he [God] does not throw dice."[5] It should not surprise anyone, therefore, that institutions, as well as noted academics, are reticent, resistant and critical of new ideas. Safety-critical industries are not impervious to these processes.

There is no shortage of institutions that lay claim to some facet of safety-critical industries. There are enforcing bodies such as the Health & Safety Executive (HSE) in the UK and the Occupational Safety and Health Administration (OSHA) in the USA. These bodies play an important role shaping the external climate that the organisational Lilypond develops within. There are also powerful professional bodies. The Institution of Occupational Safety and Health (IOSH) is the largest membership body for health and safety professionals working across 130 countries. Chartered member status with IOSH is a standard expectation for safety management roles. Likewise, recognised Human Factors qualifications are required for some to demonstrate expertise in the area. This domain is claimed by the Chartered Institute of Ergonomics and Human Factors (CIEHF). Finally, there are also professional bodies within each sector and each country such as the

General Medical Council (GMC), the Civil Aviation Authority (CAA) and the Rail Safety Standards Board (RSSB).

These institutions exist for good reason. They are also filled with people wishing to create the optimal, safe working environment. They create the "rules of the game"[6] and because there are so many strata of institutions impacting upon safety-critical industries, a map, rather than a finite solution, is the best and most appropriate conclusion to this book.

Quantum Safety is the most complete revision of organisational safety concepts for 50 years. The New View refraction (see Chapter 1) is evidence of important and helpful progression even if the propositions are incomplete. The reason why Quantum Safety can make such substantial claims, however, is that our understanding, and consequentially the approach to organisational safety, is rarely significantly different from what it was half a century ago. So why is change so limited?

The first reason why people are still heavily wedded to Newtonian Safety is that it has worked remarkably well. If our understanding of safety has remained static, workplaces are significantly safer than they were during the 1970s. People will think that excellence will occur as a result of one more push. The truth is that our modern workplace means such people are in the same predicament as polar bears on a melting ice sheet. A mentality of continuing to apply methodology as done historically, even if successful, is incongruent to a high-performance environment. Institutions therefore may not change because they consider themselves to be wining. A functionalist approach to understanding institutions suggests that they will change when they need to "in response to a change in their environment that diminishes the efficiency of existing institutions."[7] This clearly has not been the case in safety-critical industries. Olson argues that inefficient institutions may "survive for a long time because groups with stakes in institutional change fail to get organized and solve their collective action problem."[8] Additionally, "whatever group holds power will use that power in its own best interest."[8] It is not only the Catholic Church or the Prussian Academy of Sciences that will resist change from external progress. Safety-critical industries have suffered from the same malaise, protectionist intransigence and lack of intellectual curiosity too often.

Recently I spoke with an experienced safety professional within the rail sector, a Chartered member of IOSH with a PhD in Human Factors. They spoke with unshakeable confidence that the solution to a project's woes was to promote greater use of Close Calls and to utilise an LCD screen to advocate this solution to people whilst they were on a break. Whilst it would have been easy to be rather bemused with this expert, I reflected on the Bill Walsh approach of challenging the person who put them in that position to fail[9] The issue was not the person I spoke with. They were merely displaying the symptom, not the cause. Their behaviour was a result of their institutionalised, and potentially limited, professional development that rewarded adherence to specific doctrines and scriptures. If we were to analyse these institutions using the Continuum of Human & Organisational Performance, there would be as many concerning indicators as identified regarding maternity safety in Chapter 4.

Quantum Safety can be embraced as a catalyst to understand safety within an integrated approach to high performance and reform these institutions. These reforms would see a concerted shift from institutions that act as gatekeepers or sole arbiters of competency and expertise. Flexible, collaborative adaptive spaces will enable the Human Performance Foxtrot to be performed and understood at a strategic level. There would then be an institutional structure befitting this century rather than the previous one. Alternatively, Quantum Safety could of course be dismissed as heresy. History doesn't repeat, but it does rhyme after all.

12.2 Cats and Watermelons

Quantum physics has a problem. The quantum measurement problem is the paradox surrounding the impact that observation has on the state of the particle being observed.[10] This has been made famous by an imaginary cat. Edwin Schrodinger created the notorious thought experiment regarding a cat in a box. The cat is exposed to a situation where there may be a potentially lethal radioactive dose. Quantum mechanics suggests that until the box is open the cat, which could be either dead or alive, is in fact simultaneously both dead and alive until the moment of observation arrives. At that point the cat assumes one of the specific states. At a quantum level, what is seen to be occurring is not necessarily an accurate picture of reality.[5]

Among the plethora of management slogans that are perpetuated around the modern workplace, one that has caught considerable traction is "if you can't measure it, you can't manage it."[11] Safety II[12] and the Lilypond Model challenge the traditional view of what organisations understand to be their safety performance, but however broad one's view of what their organisational safety performance is there is a measurement problem. The most elementary of courses for health and safety will introduce the importance of audits as part of a safety management system. The HSE advocates "routine inspections of premises, plant and equipment by staff."[13] Such audits are considered to be an active method of checking how the safety management system is working. Safety professionals argue that they are a valuable process and they "send a clear message to the employees as a clear message that the company cares."[14] Whilst there is a clear need to be able to check the efficacy of a safety management system, there is undoubtedly a disconnect between the expectations and reality, or safety-as-imagined and safety-as-done perhaps? Olson found that a large part of the safety professional's role was writing safety policies and procedures, documenting and auditing safety management.[15] This paper-based safety approach has meant that "safety professionals have become administrators of safety bureaucracies, and their reputation among the workforce has suffered."[16] Beyond reputational damage within the workforce, this approach has become culturally toxic and can foster an environment that is not conducive to high performance.

Within Safety Differently, Sidney Dekker persuasively argues the need to counter increasing bureaucratization of safety.[17] Whilst safety management can become a "numbers game," when considering audit processes they can often become a colours game. An increasingly popular method for encapsulating routine inspections is to adopt a traffic light system. An item on the audit is given a green if it is considered acceptable, amber if there is a mild concern and red for major concern. As with most systems and measurements, this easily becomes gamified. The result is that the condition presented to the auditor is not representative of normal work conditions or activities. Work-as-done is often not being measured or checked consequently. There is often a false veneer giving the appearance of an acceptable green condition. This hides the reality behind the veneer that the substantive part of the work is actually an unacceptable state that would warrant a red denotification. The system is designed to collate things that often have a green appearance but are really substantively red. It merely collects watermelons. A false sense of security, or safety, is given and an approach to measurement which is incredibly limited as a result of a process that drives people to record an illusion of acceptability. Any system that wishes to check on its ability to manage risk must be focused truly on work-as-done. Until then, safety will continue to have its own measurement problem.

12.3 Safety Management System: The Babushka Edit

Dekker's critique of safety bureaucratization is highly welcome as is the need to consider if we need to do safety differently. Whilst rebellious or disruptive concepts are not unwelcome, Quantum Safety would fit those attributes, suggestions of anarchy are misjudged. Whether the world would be safer, or even just as safe, once we have stripped away all the road markings and signage is not the point. People simply won't do it. How many leaders in safety-critical industries would feel sufficiently empowered to start with a totally blank canvas at start again, especially when the prevailing wisdom is that the existing system is good enough, and is crucially compliant with the demands of the regulatory institutions? It would be an unacceptable risk for most.

To create a solution, therefore, which can initiate radical change within the boundaries of organisational risk tolerance is challenging. Fortunately, the solution already exists in allied fields. Safety's measurement problem can be addressed by Quality Improvement (QI) methodology.

There is no one universal definition of QI; however, it is often defined as "a systematic approach that uses specific techniques to improve quality."[18] A number of organisations amalgamate the concept of quality within the safety department, hence the oft-used acronym of SHEQ (Safety, Health, Environment and Quality). To find the solution, therefore, in quality should not be surprising. The Q of SHEQ is mostly used in consideration of the output of the task, for example, whether the school has been built well. QI focuses on understanding the process and the improvements that can be made within it. As we know, the score takes care of itself.

Healthcare is one sector that has begun to utilise QI in order to improve performance.[19] This approach has not been created within healthcare. Most of its antecedents are from industries such as manufacturing, but the way in which it is being operationalised is notably more widespread with the aim of empowering frontline teams to enact and measure the changes. For example, at Nationwide Children's Hospital NICU at the Ohio University Wexner Medical Center, a QI project set the goal of improving the rates of golden hour stabilisation at 135 minutes of life from 17% to 80% within three years. A QI project with a bundle of changes was established. The data from this intervention found that compliance increased beyond the target figure of 80%, increasing steadily from 88% to 95%.[20]

There is no one fixed method to adopt a QI approach. QI is often based on three questions: "what are we trying to achieve? How do we know if the change has made an improvement? What changes can we make that will result in an improvement?"[21] As is clear from the example from Ohio University Wexner Medical Center, the answer to the first question should not be a simplistic or idealistic safety notion such as Zero Harm. The focus should be on a specific aspect of the system.

The second question is the part that allows safety industries to move away from the fixation with collecting watermelons. Rather than suggesting a speculative colour of approval, organisations can adopt an approach based on actual data. In order to be able to observe if a change has made an improvement, there must first be a benchmark. This is usually gained from collecting at least 12 data points of the facet subject to improvement.[22] This is used to begin to formulate a run chart (see Figure 12.1). The subsequent data collected once a test of change has been implemented is considered against the median to ascertain whether the intervention has made a difference. To determine this a set of rules are applied.

The first rule considers a shift in data. If there are six or more consecutive data points on one side of the median or the other, it indicates a shift. This means that there is a less than 5% chance that this change occurred as a result of natural variation, rather than the intervention being implemented.[23] The second rule asks if there is a trend. If there are five or more data points either continually increasing or decreasing, this effect has a 3% chance of occurring naturally and not as a result of the intervention. Finally, there is the astronomical data point. If there is one data point that

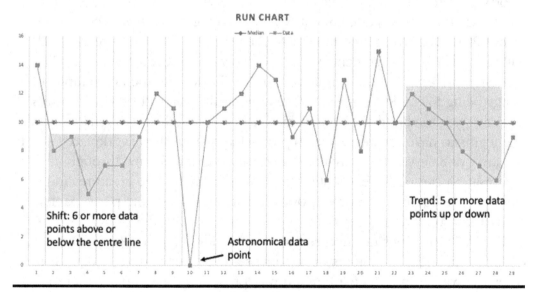

Figure 12.1   Example of a run chart for quality improvement.

is significantly different from the rest of the run this indicates activities that require further investigation.

The reader would be forgiven if they were to recognise a conceptual similarity between the use of a run chart to understand if a system is improving and the twin strands of the lily pad that encapsulate the principle of causal variation analysis (see Chapter 9), especially with the astronomical data point. There are philosophical echoes, although to make the link formal is mistaken. One important distinction being that the median line of the run chart is formed from observations of work-as-done, not work-as-imagined.

Quantum Safety also provides a mechanism for understanding the data of a run chart more effectively in complex systems. Causal variation recognises that there will be variation consistently within the system. Quality Improvement methodology proves it. The Human Performance Foxtrot (see Chapter 6) develops a nuanced approach to understanding adaptive behaviours, shifting away from a view that they are "seeds of failure." In situations that are considered to be nearer the ultra-safe part of the dance floor, the aim ought to be in reducing variation by shifting the data. In contrast, in environments where there would be more adaptive behaviours expected, reducing variation may not be the optimal goal but interventions that create trends in the data may be more helpful regarding the safety within the environment being changed.

The HSE advocates a safety management system that adopts four stages, "Plan, Do, Check, Act."[13] QI is based around the PDSA cycle. Quantum Safety incorporates these two strategies by placing QI with the Check part of a safety management system, so that we have a system that has PDSA neatly sat within Plan, Do, Check, Act like a little Babushka Doll (see Figure 12.2). This will allow safety management systems to evolve and become more flexible.

Firstly, by replacing the primary focus of Check from the appearance of things being tolerable to one of improvement, the concept of safety moves from the Newtonian to the Quantum concept. Secondly, it will enable front-line teams to have greater ownership of safety within their workplace, which is a facet of Safety Differently that has great potential. Teams throughout the organisation can become scientists of their own work. The creatures in the Lilypond are equipped to drive positive change and become participants rather than supplicants.

Crucially, this does not necessitate anarchy. It does provide evidence. Currently, changes to systems or initiatives are not supported by data. If a company was to introduce a new permit, procedure or standard, there is no mechanism to capture whether that effort has been worthwhile. The result is

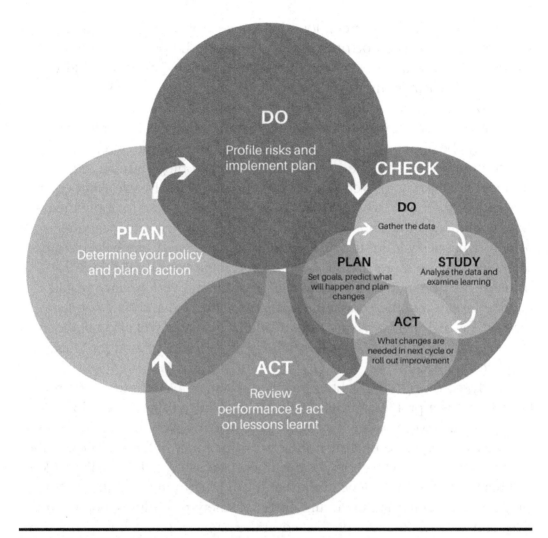

Figure 12.2   The safety management system (Babushka edit).

a Frankenstein safety management system, bloated by confusion and ava-
rice. The Babushka edit is one of radical change, but operating within the
boundaries of risk tolerance for some organisations at least. It is a marriage
of compliance and progression that, like all good unions, will create longer
and more powerful results than imagined on inception.

12.4 Rituals and Routines

The Quantum Safety world provides a significant challenge to existing structures, institutions and those that hold significant power within safety-critical

industries. The old world order, founded on Newtonian Safety, requires significant reform. The doctrines espoused need to be placed under serious critical review as to their veracity for the complex Quantum world view. Safety-related institutions should be conduits for adaptive spaces and collaboration rather than antiquated vestibules of power.

What we value should also evolve. Whilst the number of people harmed will always be an important metric, increasingly we will measure, value and communicate about the process whilst championing learning rather than merely reacting to events whilst chasing rainbows. People will become scientists of their own work. Where those scientists choose to apply their expertise in search of improvement will depend on their understanding of, and dynamics within, their Lilypond. Quantum Safety can help identify areas that may be more ripe for learning and improvement. Firstly, analysis using the Continuum of Human & Organisational Performance would provide insight into the conditions within the Lilypond and how conducive they are for high performance. Also, a true Just Culture will also help identify potential patterns of behaviour that could be fertile ground for Quality Improvement cycles.

Finally, consideration ought to be given to safety-related rituals and routines. There is a proliferation of rituals and routines in safety-critical industries. One such totem is the pre-flight safety briefing. Whether delivered via a glamorous corporate presentation or bored member of the cabin crew, the routine is observed whilst the positive impact on safety is less clear. Dekker and his team at Safety Science Innovation Lab refer to much of this as "safety clutter."[24] This clutter is the "accumulation of safety procedures, documents, roles and activities that are performed in the name of safety, but do not contribute to the safety of operations." Inductions, checklists, mandatory use of PPE and systemic duplications are all cited as possible examples of clutter.[17,24] High-performance environments cannot be reconciled with approaches that generate and protect safety clutter. Quantum Safety does not merely consider safety clutter to be unhelpful but provides an approach to remove it.

The presence of safety clutter is difficult to dispute. The effect it has on individual's perceptions of safety and the broader organisational safety culture is also clear; clutter pollutes the organisational Lilypond. Irrespective of their professionalism, people are often reluctant to tackle the problem of rituals and routines. It is easier to add to a risk management system. It is more challenging to remove items from it. This is understandable in safety-critical industries and the need to comply with regulators. People feel the need to be seen to be managing safely. The fact that adding to a system does not equate to improvement and removing items doesn't automatically increase risk is often lost. Consequently, in order to create radical change, the answer is not found by advocating safety anarchists as this requires a leap of faith most wouldn't feel able to countenance. The route to serious improvement is with helping people become scientists of their own work. The PDSA cycles of Quality Improvement should be integrated into an organisations approach to checking their safety performance, consistently and scientifically.

This approach also enables localised adaptation to replace global rules. Organisations can generate routines and rituals following adverse events. Whilst well meaning, they can often create peculiar or nonsensical situations where people planting flowers require a permit and a person stood in the middle of a field is mandated to wear a safety helmet. Changes made that span an entire organisation may make it easier for a risk management system to monitor compliance. It does not, however, necessarily correlate to effective safety management or an improvement in performance. Local groups, by becoming scientists of their own work, can create tests of change and demonstrate that any proposed adaptations act as improvements to performance.

This approach will also serve as an effective check or balance to the issue of transplanting safety. Innovations or approaches that are deemed to improve safety can quickly disseminate around an industry or between sectors. For example, many organisations within construction, rail and other high-risk industries adopt a policy of mandatory reverse parking. It has become a way to signal a safety virtue. The demonstrable impact this rule has on people's safety is unclear, although it is interesting to consider, if such evidence was available and overwhelming, why would other industries such as supermarkets insist on this improvement to safety? The use of checklists is another example, as Lucian Leape identified "there is considerable evidence that they can be very effective, but also evidence that they are sometimes not effective at all."[25]

The issue arises from people attempting to transplant an idea from another environment. This demonstrates a fundamental lack of understanding of systemic dynamics as people suggest the route to improving performance within a construction company requires the same approach as an oil rig or a hospital equivalent to an aircraft. It is a result of applying linear thinking to complex problems. Collaboration should be welcomed, but ideas should be analysed to how they may translate, not transplant, into different situations. A deep consideration of the Human Performance Foxtrot (see Chapter 6) may be helpful with this endeavour; what kind of dance are we learning from? What part of the three-stage dance floor are we operating? and how similar are the dynamics between the two parties that are learning from one another?

12.5 The Quantum Safety Roadmap

The roadmap of Quantum Safety offers a range of overlays that convey information to help people and organisations arrive at their destination. Safety approaches dictated by intransigent behemoths and managed by reactionary, limited systems are a legacy of our Newtonian past. A future based on the principles of Quantum Safety is attainable at all levels, from the political to the frontline teams, all empowered to create the conditions that enable high performance through improvements based on data rather than doctrines. How people chose to navigate through the complexity of their own organisations towards that goal is the true science of work.

Questions for Reflection

1. What are the routines, rituals and patterns of behaviour that may provide scope for improvement?
2. What would you like to have as part of your roadmap to a Quantum Safety future?

References

1. Miller JH & Page SE. (2007). *Complex Adaptive Systems: An introduction to computational models of social life.* Princeton University Press.
2. Uhl-Bien, M & Arena, M. (2017). Complexity leadership: Enabling people and organisations for adaptability. *Organizational Dynamics*, 46(1): 9–20.
3. Boisot, M & Mckelvey, B. (2011). Complexity and organization-environment relations: revisiting Ashby's law of requisite variety. In Peter Allen, Steve Maguire & Bill McKelvey (eds.), *The Sage Handbook of Complexity and Management.* Sage Publications. pp. 279–298.
4. Leveillee, NP. (2011). Copernicus, Galilleo and the Church: Science in a religious world. *Inquiries Journal: Social Sciences, Arts & Humanities.* [online] Available at: http://www.inquiriesjournal.com/articles/1675/copernicus-galileo-and-the-church-science-in-a-religious-world [Accessed 06.04.21].
5. Al-Khalili J. (2017). *Quantum Mechanics.* Penguin.

6. North, D. (1990). *Institutions, Institutional Change and Economic Performance,* Cambridge University Press.

7. Roland G. (2008). Fast moving and slow moving institutions. In Kornai J, Matyas L & Roland G (eds.), *Institutional Change and Economic Behaviour. International Economic Association Series.* Palgrave Macmillan. https://doi.org/10.1057/9780230583429_7

8. Olson, M. (1982). *The Rise and Decline of Nations: Economic Growth, Stagflation and Social Rigidities.* Yale University Press.

9. Walsh B, Jamison S & Walsh C. (2009). *The Score Takes Care of Itself: My Philosophy of Leadership.* Penguin.

10. De Ronde C. (2020). The (quantum) measurement problem in classical mechanics. Submitted at Cornell University. [online] Available at: https://arxiv.org/pdf/2001.00241.pdf [Accessed 10.04.21].

11. Prince, M. (2018). "If you can't measure it, you can't manage it": Essential truth or costly myth? *World Psychiatry* [online] Available at: https://www.ncbi.nlm.nih.gov/pmc/articles/PMC5775130/ [Accessed 10.04.21].

12. Hollnagel, E. (2014). *Safety-I and Safety-II. The Past and Future of Safety Management.* CRC Press.

13. The Health & Safety Executive. (2013). *Managing for Health & Safety.* [online] Available at: https://www.hse.gov.uk/pubns/priced/hsg65.pdf [Accessed 10.04.21].

14. Schiavi AR. (2014). Safety audits as leading indicators. *Professional Safety,* 59(4). [online] Available at: https://search.proquest.com/openview/f48f5c66600aff38b50a33c1ccf06c7c/1?pq-origsite=gscholar&cbl=47267 [Accessed 10.04.21].

15. Olsen, K. (2014). OHS Practitioners' Role in implementation of national OHS programmes. Nordic Ergonomics Society Annual Conference: 385–391.

16. Provan D & Rae A. (2017). Bureaucracy, influence and beliefs: A literature review of the factors shaping the role of a safety professional. *Safety Science.* [online] Available at URL: https://www.researchgate.net/profile/David-Provan/publication/317694732_Bureaucracy_influence_and_beliefs_A_literature_review_of_the_factors_shaping_the_role_of_a_safety_professional/links/59d600ccaca2725954c7a3b8/Bureaucracy-influence-and-beliefs-A-literature-review-of-the-factors-shaping-the-role-of-a-safety-professional.pdf [Accessed 10.04.21].

17. Dekker SWA. (2014). The bureaucratization of safety. *Safety Science,* 70(348): 357 [online] Available at: https://www.safetydifferently.com/wp-content/uploads/2014/08/BureaucratizationSafety.pdf [Accessed 11.04.21].

18. Jones, B, Kwong E & Warburton W. (2021). Quality improvement made simple. What everyone should know about the health care quality improvement. The Health Foundation. [online] Available at: https://www.health.org.uk/sites/default/files/QualityImprovementMadeSimple.pdf [Accessed 10.04.21]

19. Bergman B, Hellstrom A, Lifvergren S & Gustavsson S. (2015). An emerging science of improvement in health care. *Quality Engineering.* [online] Available at: http://www.vinnvard.se/files/2714/4016/1583/An_emerging_science_of_improvement_in_health_care_2014.pdf [Accessed 12.04.21].

20. Habib A, Leukart RL, Bartman T & Schlegel A. (2016). Bundles overcome hurdles in the golden hour for <28 week neonates. *BMJ Quality & Safety*, 25: 999–1000.

21. Langley GL, Moen R, Nolan KM, Nolan TW, Norman CL & Provost LP. (2009). *The Improvement Guide: A Practical Approach to Enhancing Organizational Performance* (2nd ed.). Jossey-Bass Publishers.

22. Provost, L. & S. Murray. (2011). *The Health Care Data Guide*. Jossey-Bass.

23. Lloyd, R. (2010). Navigating in the turbulent sea of data: The quality measurement journey. Special edition on quality improvement in neonatology and perinatal medicine. *Clinics in Perinatology*, 37(1): 101–122.

24. Rae AJ, Provan DJ, Weber DE & Dekker SWA. (2020). Safety clutter: The accumulation and persistence of 'safety' work that does not contribute to operational safety. [online] Available at: ⟨https://www.nzism.org/crm/file/user/2/uploads/Safety%20Clutter%20Preprint.pdf [Accessed 20.04.21].

25. Leape LL. (2014). The checklist conundrum. *New England Journal of Medicine*, 370(11), 1063–1064.

Index

Printed in the United States
by Baker & Taylor Publisher Services